English

An Essential Grammar

2nd Edition

Gerald Nelson

Routledge
Taylor & Francis Group

LONDON AND NEW YORK

First edition published 2001
by Routledge

This second edition first published 2011
by Routledge
2 Park Square, Milton Park, Abingdon, Oxon OX14 4RN

Simultaneously published in the USA and Canada
by Routledge
711 Third Ave, New York, NY 10017

Routledge is an imprint of the Taylor & Francis Group, an informa business

© 2001, 2011 Gerald Nelson

The right of Gerald Nelson to be identified as author of this work has
been asserted by him in accordance with sections 77 and 78 of the
Copyright, Designs and Patents Act 1988.

Typeset in Sabon and Gill by
Florence Production Ltd, Stoodleigh, Devon

British Library Cataloguing in Publication Data
A catalogue record for this book is available from the British Library

Library of Congress Cataloging in Publication Data
Nelson, Gerald, 1959–
English : an essential grammar / Gerald Nelson. — [2nd ed.].
   p. cm. — (Routledge essential grammars)
   Includes bibliographical references and index.
   1. English language—Grammar. I. Title.
   PE1112.N45 2011
   428.2—dc22   2010019803

ISBN13: 978–0–415–58295–7 (hbk)
ISBN13: 978–0–415–58296–4 (pbk)
ISBN13: 978–0–203–84938–5 (ebk)

English

_01264 360050_

An Essential Grammar

2nd Edition

English: An Essential Grammar is a concise and user-friendly guide to the grammar of modern English, written specifically for native speakers and based on genuine samples of contemporary spoken and written English.

In the first four chapters, this book covers the essentials of English grammar, beginning with the basics and going on to deal with phrase, clause and sentence structure. A fifth chapter deals with English word formation and spelling, including problem spellings and British and American spelling variants.

Features include:

- discussion of points that often cause problems
- guidance on sentence building and composition
- practical spelling guidelines
- explanation of grammatical terms
- a set of exercises at the end of each chapter
- appendix of irregular verbs.

With numerous language examples bringing grammar to life, this _Essential Grammar_ will help you read, speak and write English with greater confidence. It is ideal for everyone who would like to improve their knowledge of English grammar.

Gerald Nelson is Professor in the English Department at The Chinese University of Hong Kong, and was formerly Reader in the Department of English Language and Literature, University College London, UK.

Routledge Essential Grammars

Essential Grammars are available for the following languages:

Arabic
Chinese
Czech
Danish
Dutch
English
Finnish
Georgian
German
Modern Greek
Modern Hebrew
Hindi
Hungarian
Korean
Latvian (forthcoming)
Norwegian
Polish
Portuguese
Romanian
Serbian
Spanish
Swedish
Thai
Turkish
Urdu

Contents

Chapter 5   Word formation and spelling

Introduction

Grammar is the study of how words combine to form sentences. The following is a well-formed, 'grammatical' sentence:

1 John has been ill.

Native speakers of English can produce and understand a sentence such as this without ever thinking about its grammar. Conversely, no native speaker of English would ever produce a sentence like this:

2 *[1]ill John been has.

This is an ill-formed, 'ungrammatical' sentence. But can you say why?

The study of grammar provides us with the terminology we need to talk about language in an informed way. It enables us to analyse and to describe our own use of language, as well as that of other people. In writing, a knowledge of grammar enables us to evaluate the choices that are available to us during composition.

Grammar rules

Many people think of grammar in terms of the traditional rules, such as 'Never split an infinitive' or 'Never end a sentence with a preposition'. Specifically, these are prescriptive rules, and they were designed to provide guidelines for writers of formal prose. In that sense, they are useful enough, though they tell us little, if anything, about how English is really used in everyday life. In fact, native speakers regularly split infinitives (*to boldly go*), and sentences often end with a preposition (*Dr Brown is the man I'll vote for*).

---

1 An asterisk is used throughout this book to indicate ungrammatical or incorrect examples that are used to illustrate a point.

Prescriptive grammar reached its peak in the nineteenth century. In the twenty-first century, grammarians try to adopt a more descriptive approach. In the descriptive approach, the rules of grammar – the ones that concern us in this book – are the rules that native speakers of English follow every time they speak. For instance, when we say *John has been ill*, we follow several grammar rules, including rules about:

1 where to place the Subject *John* – before the verb (see section **1.2**);
2 Subject–verb agreement – *John has*, not *John have* (see section **1.3**);
3 verb forms – *been*, not *being* (see section **2.3.1**).

Standard English

Standard English is the variety of English that carries the greatest social prestige in a speech community. In Britain, there is a standard British English; in the United States, there is a standard American English; in Australia, a standard Australian English; and so on. In each country, the national standard is that variety which is used in public institutions, including government, education, the judiciary and the media. It is used on national television and radio, and in newspapers, books and magazines. The standard variety is the only variety that has a standardised spelling. As a result, the national standard has the widest currency as a means of communication, in contrast with regional varieties, which have a more limited currency.

The following sentence is an example of standard English:

I *was* ill last week.

The following sentence is non-standard:

I *were* ill last week.

The non-standard past-tense construction *I were* is commonly used in several regional varieties, especially in parts of England. Regional varieties are associated with particular regions. The standard variety is not geographically bound in the same way.

Using standard English involves making choices of grammar, vocabulary and spelling. It has nothing to do with accent. The sentence *I was ill last week* is standard English, whether it is spoken with a Birmingham accent, a Glasgow accent, a Cockney accent, a Newcastle accent, or any other of the many accents in Britain today. Similarly, standard American English (sometimes called 'General American') is used throughout the United States, from San Francisco to New York, from New Orleans to the Great Lakes.

In both countries, the standard variety co-exists with a very large number of regional varieties. In fact, most educated people use both their own regional variety and the standard variety, and they can switch effortlessly between the two. They usually speak both varieties with the same accent.

No variety of English – including standard English – is inherently better or worse than any other. However, the standard variety is the one that has the greatest value, in social terms, as a means of communication, especially for public and professional communication. The notion of standard English is especially important to learners of the language. Because of its high social value, learners are justifiably anxious to ensure that the English they learn is standard English.

English as a world language

Conservative estimates put the total number of English speakers throughout the world at around 800 million. English is the mother tongue of an estimated 380 million people in the countries listed below.

In addition to these countries, English is an official language, or has special status, in over sixty countries worldwide, including Cameroon, Ghana, India, Jamaica, Kenya, Nigeria, Tanzania, Pakistan, the Philippines and Singapore. This means that English is used in these countries in many public functions, including government, the judiciary, the press and broadcasting. Even in countries where it has no official status, such as China and Japan, English has a central place in the school curriculum, because its importance in international communication and trade is unquestioned.

Approximate number of mother-tongue English speakers, in millions	
United States	270
Great Britain	60
Canada	17
Australia	20
New Zealand	4
Ireland	4
South Africa	2

The spread of English around the world was one of the most significant linguistic developments of the twentieth century. That century also witnessed another important development: the decline of British English and the rise of American English as the dominant variety.

British English and American English

Linguistic influence follows closely on political and economic influence. For several centuries, British English was the dominant variety throughout the world, because Britain was the centre of a vast empire that straddled the globe. In the twentieth century, political power shifted dramatically away from Britain, and, since the end of the Second World War, the United States has been, both politically and economically, the most powerful country in the world. It is not surprising then that American English has become the dominant variety, although the traditional influence of British English remains strong. In recent years, the worldwide influence of American English has been greatly strengthened by the mass media and the entertainment industry. American news channels such as CNN and NBC are transmitted around the world by satellite, and American movies and television shows are seen on almost every continent. The English used on the Internet is overwhelmingly American English.

The differences between American English and British English are, for the most part, fairly superficial. Perhaps the most familiar differences are in vocabulary:

British English	American English
autumn	fall
film	movie
flat	apartment
holiday	vacation
lift	elevator
nappy	diaper
number plate	license plate
petrol	gas
post code	zip code
rubbish	trash
shop	store
tap	faucet
taxi	cab
trainers	sneakers

Some of the American English words on this list – particularly *apartment, cab* and *movie* – are slowly being assimilated into British English. No doubt this trend will continue. International communication and travel tend to smooth the differences between national varieties, in favour of the dominant variety.

In the spoken language, there are very noticeable differences in stress between American English and British English. For instance, American speakers generally stress the final syllable in *adult*, while British speakers stress the first syllable: a<u>dult</u>. Other stress differences include the following (the stressed syllables are underlined):

British English	American English
ad<u>dress</u>	<u>ad</u>dress
<u>bal</u>let	bal<u>let</u>
cigar<u>ette</u>	<u>ci</u>garette
<u>de</u>bris	de<u>bris</u>
<u>ga</u>rage	ga<u>rage</u>
lab<u>o</u>ratory	<u>lab</u>oratory
maga<u>zine</u>	<u>ma</u>gazine

Finally, spelling differences include:

British English	American English
cheque	check
humour	humor
pyjamas	pajamas
plough	plow
theatre	theater
tyre	tire

For more on spelling differences, see section **5.13**.

The grammatical differences between American English and British English are far less obvious. They tend to be localised in very specific areas of grammar. Some differences may be observed in the use of **prepositions** (see section **2.8**). For example, Americans say *ten after twelve*, while Britons say *ten past twelve;* Americans say *in back of the house,* while Britons say *behind the house.* In the choice of verb forms, too, we can see some systematic differences. American English tends to prefer the regular form of a verb when a choice is available: for example, *burned* in favour of *burnt, learned* in favour of *learnt* (see section **2.3.8**).

Despite their differences, American English and British English, as well as all the other national varieties – Australian, Canadian, New Zealand, Indian and so on – share a very extensive, common core of vocabulary, spelling and grammar. It is this common core that makes them mutually intelligible. In this book, we are concerned with the core grammatical features of English, and especially with the core features of the two major varieties, American English and British English.

The grammatical hierarchy

The building blocks of grammar are sentences, clauses, phrases and words. These four units constitute what is called the grammatical hierarchy. We can represent the hierarchy schematically, as shown here:

SENTENCES
  – consist of one or more:
    CLAUSES
      – consist of one or more:
        PHRASES
          – consist of one or more:
            WORDS

Sentences are at the top of the grammatical hierarchy, and so they are often the largest units to be considered in a grammar book. However, in this book, we also look briefly at some of the devices that are available for joining sentences to other sentences, and for organising them in continuous discourse. These topics are discussed later in the book; see section **4.11**.

In Chapter 1, we look at sentences in terms of their sentence 'elements' – Subject, verb, Object etc. In Chapter 2, we turn our attention to the lower end of the hierarchy and consider how words are classified into word classes. The following two chapters look at phrases and clauses, respectively.

Words are at the bottom of the hierarchy, and for that reason some grammar books treat them as the smallest units in a language. However, the internal structure of a word can often play an important role. For instance, when we add the inflection *-er* to the adjective *old,* we create the comparative adjective *older*. In Chapter 5, we look at the internal structure of words, and especially at prefixes and suffixes. We also look at some of the methods that are available for creating new words, including 'blending' – combining parts of words, such as '*cam*' (from *camera*) and '*corder*' (from *recorder*), to create the new word *camcorder*. Chapter 5 concludes by looking at English spelling. It offers general rules for spelling and discusses some common spelling problems – words such as *affect* and *effect*, which are easily and regularly confused with each other in writing.

Form and function in grammatical description

In this grammar, the approach to grammatical description is the Form–Function Approach. 'Form' refers to the 'shape' or 'appearance' of a sentence element. For example, in the following sentence:

The old man fed his dog.

we say that *the old man* has the **form** of a noun phrase (see section **3.2**), because its main word, *man*, is a noun.

We can also describe *the old man* in terms of its **function**, that is, the role that it plays in the sentence as a whole. In this case, we say that *the old man* has the function of Subject (see section **1.3**). So, in the Form–Function Approach, we say that *the old man* is a noun phrase (form), which is the Subject (function) of the sentence. Following the same approach, we can say that *his dog* also has the form of a noun phrase, but it has a different function: it plays the role of Direct Object (see section **1.3**) in the sentence.

To understand the Form–Function Approach, it is perhaps useful to think in terms of actors and roles. In the sentence above, the 'actor' is the noun phrase *the old man*, playing the role of Subject. In another sentence, the same actor could play a different role. For example, in *We met the old man*, the role played by *the old man* is Direct Object.

In order to highlight the distinction between form and function, I have adopted the convention, in this grammar, of spelling form terms with a lower-case initial (e.g. noun, noun phrase, adjective) and function terms with an upper-case initial (e.g. Subject, Direct Object).

Chapter 1

The basic sentence elements

1.1   Simple, compound and complex sentences

In writing, a sentence is any sequence of words that begins with a capital letter and ends with a full stop (period), a question mark or an exclamation mark:

Paul plays football.

Amy prefers tennis.

Who lives in the house next door?

Where did you buy your car?

What a silly thing to say!

How big you've grown!

These are all **simple sentences**. We can combine two simple sentences using *but* or *and*:

1   Paul plays football.
2   Amy prefers tennis.
3   Paul plays football *but/and* Amy prefers tennis.

A combination, such as 3, which consists of two or more simple sentences, is called a **compound sentence**.

A **complex sentence** contains another 'sentence-like' construction within it:

When the plane landed, the ground crew removed the cargo.

Here, the sentence as a whole contains the 'sentence-like' construction *When the plane landed*. It is 'sentence-like' in that it has its own Subject, *the plane*, and its own **verb**, *landed*. We refer to this construction as a **clause**:

Sentence

$\longleftarrow\hspace{10em}\longrightarrow$

Clause

$\longleftarrow\hspace{5em}\longrightarrow$

When the plane landed   the ground crew removed the cargo.

We will discuss clauses, as well as complex sentences, in Chapter 4. In this chapter, we concentrate on simple sentences.

1.2   Subject and Predicate

Typically, a simple sentence consists of a **Subject** and a **Predicate**. The Subject is usually the first element in the sentence, while the rest of the sentence, which includes the verb, is the Predicate. Here are some examples of Subjects and Predicates:

Subject	Predicate
Amy	laughed.
Paul	plays football.
The house	is very old.
The detectives	interviewed the suspects.

The Predicate always contains at least a verb. In these examples, the verbs are *laughed*, *plays*, *is* and *interviewed*.

1.3   Identifying the Subject

The Subject (S) of a sentence can often be identified by asking a question beginning with *who* or *what*:

Amy laughed.
Q: *Who* laughed?
A: *Amy* (= Subject)

The house is very old.
Q: *What* is very old?
A: *The house* (= Subject)

The Subject of a sentence can also be identified using the following tests:

1   **The inversion test.** In a declarative sentence (a statement – see section **1.15.1**), the Subject (S) comes before the verb (V):

> **Declarative**: James (S) is (V) at school.

When we change this to an interrogative sentence (a question – see section **1.15.2**), the Subject and the verb change places (invert) with each other:

> **Interrogative**: Is (V) James (S) at school?

2   **The tag question test.** A **tag question** (see section **4.7.3**) is a question that is added to the end of a statement:

> Paul is getting big, *isn't he?*

The Subject of the tag question refers back to the Subject of the statement, and in that way helps us to identify the Subject of the sentence as a whole. In this example, *he* refers back to *Paul*, and so *Paul* is the Subject of the sentence.

Similarly:

> *The children* seem busy, don't *they?*

Here, *they* refers back to *the children*, and so *the children* is the Subject of the sentence.

The tag question test can also be used to identify the Subject of more difficult sentences:

> *It* was Paul who sent the note, wasn't *it?*

Here, the tag question test identifies the Subject of the sentence as *it* (see section **4.17**).

3   **The agreement test.** The Subject of a sentence agrees in number (singular or plural) with the verb that follows it. Compare:

> **Singular Subject**:   *The dog barks all night.*
>
> **Plural Subject**:   *The dogs bark all night.*

Here, the form of the verb (*barks* or *bark*) is determined by whether the Subject is singular (*the dog*) or plural (*the dogs*). This is known as **Subject–verb agreement**.

However, Subject–verb agreement only applies when the verb has a present-tense form. In the past tense, there is no agreement with the Subject:

Singular Subject: *The dog barked* all night.

Plural Subject: *The dogs barked* all night.

Furthermore, agreement applies only to third-person Subjects. For instance, the same verb form is used whether the Subject is *I* (the first-person singular) or *we* (the first-person plural):

Singular Subject: *I sleep* all night.

Plural Subject: *We sleep* all night.

For these reasons, the agreement test can only be used to identify the Subject of a sentence when the Subject is third person, and when the verb has present-tense form.

1.4   Verb types

The pattern of a simple sentence is largely determined by the type of verb it contains. There are three verb types: intransitive (see section **1.4.1**), linking (see section **1.4.2**) and transitive (see section **1.4.3**).

1.4.1   *Intransitive verbs*

An **intransitive verb** can occur alone in the Predicate of a sentence, because it requires no other sentence element to complete its meaning:

Amy *laughed.*

The baby *cried.*

The temperature *dropped.*

The sky *darkened.*

The ship *disappeared.*

Each of these sentences contains just a Subject and a verb, and so their pattern is:

Sentence Pattern 1:

```
S          V
Amy        laughed.
```

1.4.2 | *Linking verbs*

Unlike other verbs (such as *destroy, sing, laugh, eat, break*), the verb *be* does not denote any kind of 'action'. Instead, it links the Subject to another element following the verb:

Paul *is* 12.

Here, we would not say that Paul performs any 'action' in 'being 12'. The verb simply links the two elements *Paul* and *12*, and, for that reason, we call it a **linking verb**.

Be is by far the most common linking verb, though there are several others:

David *seems* unhappy.

The house *appeared* empty.

She *looks* uncomfortable.

The animals *became* restless.

The crowd *went* wild.

The element following a linking verb is called the **Subject Complement** (SC – see section **1.5**). Therefore the pattern in these sentences is:

Sentence Pattern 2:

S	V	SC
Paul	is	12.

1.4.3 | *Transitive verbs*

A **transitive verb** is a verb that cannot stand alone in the Predicate of a sentence. Instead, it requires another sentence element to complete its meaning. Consider, for example, the verb *destroy*. This verb needs an element following it – one cannot simply *destroy*, one has to destroy *something*. Compare:

*The soldiers destroyed.

The soldiers destroyed the village.

Destroy, therefore, is a transitive verb. Further examples of transitive verbs include:

The generator *produces* electricity.

Jim *bought* a new house.

She really *enjoyed* her party.

Christopher Wren *designed* St Paul's Cathedral.

In these examples, the element that completes the meaning of the transitive verb (*the village, electricity, a new house* etc.) is called the **Direct Object** (DO – see section **1.6**). These sentences therefore display the pattern:

Sentence Pattern 3:

S	V	DO
The soldiers	destroyed	the village.

Many verbs have both intransitive (see section **1.4.1**) and transitive uses, sometimes with different meanings. Compare the following pairs:

Intransitive: *The children grew* (S + V)

Transitive: The children grew flowers (S + V + DO)

Intransitive: *The old man shook* (S + V)

Transitive: The old man shook his fist (S + V + DO)

Intransitive: *Simon has changed* (S + V)

Transitive: Simon has changed his clothes (S + V + DO)

1.5   Subject Complement

When the verb in a sentence is a linking verb, such as *be, seem, appear* (see section **1.4.2**), the element following the verb is called the Subject Complement (SC):

Paul is *12*.

The Subject Complement typically denotes an attribute or property of the Subject. In this example, it denotes the age of the Subject, *Paul*. Here are some more examples of Subject Complements:

Subject	Complement
My tea is	*cold.*
Mr Johnson is	*an engineer.*
The house appeared	*empty.*
He became	*Prime Minister.*

1.6　Direct Object

In the sentence *The soldiers destroyed the village*, we refer to the element *the village* as the Direct Object (DO). The DO is required to complete the meaning of the verb *destroyed*. Here are some more examples of sentences with DOs:

	Direct Object
The detectives interviewed	*the suspects.*
This shop sells	*excellent bread.*
The storm caused	*a lot of damage.*

The DO is typically that part of a sentence which is affected by the 'action' of the verb. It can often be identified by asking a question beginning with *what* or *whom*:

The soldiers destroyed the village.
Q: *What* did the soldiers destroy?
A: The village (= DO)

The detectives interviewed the suspects.
Q: *Whom* did the detectives interview?
A: The suspects (= DO)

1.7　Indirect Object

Some sentences contain two **Objects**:

We gave David the prize.

The two Objects here are *David* and *the prize*. The element *the prize* is the Direct Object (*What did we give David? – The prize*). The other Object, *David*, is called the **Indirect Object** (IO). Here are some more examples of sentences with two Objects:

	Indirect Object	**Direct Object**
They awarded	*James*	*a salary increase.*
She told	*her husband*	*the news.*
I asked	*him*	*a question.*
The postman brought	*us*	*a package.*

When two Objects are present in a sentence, the Indirect Object comes first, followed by the Direct Object, so the pattern is:

Sentence Pattern 4:

S	V	IO	DO
We	gave	David	the prize.

Pattern 4 sentences can often be rewritten as follows:

We gave David the prize.

~[1] We gave the prize to David.

1.8   Object Complement

An **Object Complement** (OC) describes an attribute of the Direct Object (see section **1.6**):

The dye turned the water *blue*.

Here, *blue* is the Object Complement. It describes an attribute (the colour) of *the water*, which is the Direct Object. Here are some more examples:

His comments made me *angry* (OC).

They elected Amy *Treasurer* (OC).

Mary called Simon *a fool* (OC).

Object Complements occur after the Object that they describe, and so the pattern in these sentences is:

Sentence Pattern 5:

S	V	DO	OC
The dye	turned	the water	blue.

At first glance, some Pattern 5 sentences may look very similar to Pattern 4 sentences. Compare:

1 **Pattern 5:**

S	V	DO	OC
The manager	made	Jones	*captain*.

2 **Pattern 4:**

S	V	IO	DO
The manager	made	Jones	*coffee*.

---

1 The symbol ~ is used throughout this book to mean 'may legitimately be changed to'.

The grammatical difference between these two can be seen when we rephrase them. Sentence 2 can be rephrased as:

2a The manager made coffee *for Jones.*

In contrast, sentence 1 cannot be rephrased in the same way:

1a *The manager made captain *for Jones.*

The element *captain* in sentence 1 describes an attribute of *Jones* ('Jones is captain'), and so *captain* is an Object Complement.

Similarly, compare:

Pattern 5: Mary called Simon *a fool.* ('Simon is a fool.')

Pattern 4: Mary called Simon *a taxi.* ('Mary called a taxi for Simon.')

1.9 Adverbial Complement

In section 1.4.1, we saw that intransitive verbs require no other sentence element to complete their meaning. However, some intransitive verbs co-occur with a sentence element that expresses location, direction or time, and that is obligatory in the sentence structure:

This road goes *to Sevenoaks.*

The farm lies *about a mile east of town.*

On Broadway, the play ran *for six months.*

The meeting lasted *two hours.*

In each of these examples, the verb is intransitive, and yet the element that follows it is required to complete the meaning. This required element is called the **Adverbial Complement** (AC).

1.10 The six sentence patterns

In the previous sections, we looked at the following sentence elements:

Subject	S	(see section **1.3**)
Verb	V	(see section **1.4**)
Subject Complement	SC	(see section **1.5**)
Direct Object	DO	(see section **1.6**)
Indirect Object	IO	(see section **1.7**)
Object Complement	OC	(see section **1.8**)
Adverbial Complement	AC	(see section **1.9**)

These elements combine to form the six basic sentence patterns shown in Table 1.1.

Table 1.1 Sentence patterns and verb types

Sentence pattern	Verb type	Examples
1 S + V	Intransitive	Amy (S) *laughed* (V).
		The audience (S) *applauded* (V).
		The temperature (S) *dropped* (V).
2 S + V + SC	Linking	My tea (S) *is* (V) *cold* (SC).
		My friend (S) *is* (V) *ill* (SC).
		David (S) *seems* (V) *unhappy* (SC).
3 S + V + DO	Transitive	The soldiers (S) *destroyed* (V) *the village* (DO).
		The police (S) *interviewed* (V) *the suspects* (DO).
		The storm (S) *caused* (V) *a lot of damage* (DO).
4 S + V + IO + DO	Transitive	We (S) *gave* (V) *David* (IO) *the prize* (DO).
		They (S) *awarded* (V) *James* (IO) *a salary increase* (DO).
		I (S) *asked* (V) *him* (IO) *a question* (DO).
5 S + V + DO + OC	Transitive	The dye (S) *turned* (V) *the water* (DO) *blue* (OC).
		His comments (S) *made* (V) *me* (DO) *angry* (OC).
		They (S) *elected* (V) *Amy* (DO) *President* (OC).
6 S + V + AC	Intransitive	This road (S) *goes* (V) *to Sevenoaks* (AC)
		The farm (S) *lies* (V) *about a mile east of the town* (AC)
		The meeting (S) *lasted* (V) *two hours* (AC)

Key: AC = Adverbial Complement; DO = Direct Object; IO = Indirect Object; OC = Object Complement; S = Subject; SC = Subject Complement; V = verb

Notice that the elements S (Subject) and V (verb) are present in all the patterns. This means that all sentences contain at least a Subject and a verb. There is one exception to this: imperative sentences such as *Look!* and *Move over!* have a verb, but no Subject (see section **1.15.3**).

1.11 Active sentences and passive sentences

Sentences are either **active** or **passive**.

> **Active**:   Shakespeare *wrote* King Lear.
>
> **Passive**:   King Lear *was written* by Shakespeare.

The active sentence has the pattern S + V + DO (Pattern 3 – see Table 1.1). The Direct Object *King Lear* becomes the Subject of the passive version, while *Shakespeare*, the Subject of the active version, moves to the end of the passive version.

Passive sentences are formed by adding the passive auxiliary *be* (see section **2.7.3**) and by using a different form of the verb – in this case *written* instead of *wrote*. On the verb forms, see section **2.3.1**.

Here are some more examples of active and passive pairs:

> **Active**:   The burglar broke a pane of glass.
>
> **Passive**:   A pane of glass was broken by the burglar.
>
> **Active**:   The curator shows the manuscript to visitors.
>
> **Passive**:   The manuscript is shown to visitors by the curator.
>
> **Active**:   The police interviewed the witnesses.
>
> **Passive**:   The witnesses were interviewed by the police.

The '*by*-phrase' (*by the burglar*, *by the curator*, *by the police*) is sometimes omitted, leaving an **agentless passive**:

> **Active**:   The burglar broke a pane of glass.
>
> **Passive**:   A pane of glass was broken by the burglar.
>
> **Agentless passive**:   A pane of glass was broken.

Only sentences with a transitive verb (see section **1.4.3**) can have a passive version. However, a small number of verbs cannot be passivised, even though they are transitive in the active version. These include *have*, *resemble* and *suit*:

Active:	James *has* a new car.
Passive:	*A new car is *had* by James.
Active:	Paul *resembles* Anthony.
Passive:	*Anthony *is resembled* by Paul.
Active:	That colour *suits* you.
Passive:	*You *are suited* by that colour.

The distinction between an active sentence and a passive sentence is called voice.

1.12 Adjuncts

The six sentence patterns (Table 1.1) can all be extended by the use of **Adjuncts**. Adjuncts (A) contribute optional, additional information to a sentence. For example, the S + V sentence *The sky darkened* can be extended, by the addition of Adjuncts, to become:

The sky darkened *suddenly*. (S + V + A)

The sky darkened *before the hailstorm*. (S + V + A)

The sky darkened *at about 9 o'clock*. (S + V + A)

In the following examples, we show how each of the six sentence patterns may be extended by adding an Adjunct:

Pattern 1: S + V + A
Amy laughed *loudly* (A).

Pattern 2: S + V + SC + A
My tea is cold *as usual* (A).

Pattern 3: S + V + DO + A
The soldiers destroyed the village *deliberately* (A).

Pattern 4: S + V + IO + DO + A
We gave David the prize *in the end* (A).

Pattern 5: S + V + DO + OC + A
The dye turned the water blue *in just a few seconds* (A).

Pattern 6: S + V + AC + A
The meeting lasted two hours, *unfortunately* (A).

19

Adjuncts can also appear at the beginning of a sentence, before the Subject:

Suddenly, the sky darkened. (A+S+V)

Before the hailstorm, the sky darkened. (A+S+V)

At about 9 o'clock, the sky darkened. (A+S+V)

And, finally, Adjuncts can co-occur. That is, more than one Adjunct can occur in the same sentence:

Before the hailstorm (A), the sky darkened *suddenly* (A).

Unfortunately (A), my tea is cold *as usual* (A).

On Sunday (A), *after the game* (A), we met Simon *outside the stadium* (A).

In contrast with this, a simple sentence can contain just one Subject, one verb, one Direct Object and so on.

1.13 The meanings of Adjuncts

Adjuncts (see section **1.12**) contribute various types of additional information to a sentence. The principal information types are set out below.

1   **Time** (*when* something happens):

The play opened *yesterday*.

Our guests arrived *at seven o'clock*.

We visit Greece *every year*.

2   **Place** (*where* something happens):

Amy attended university *in New York*.

We met Simon *outside the restaurant*.

I saw David *at the swimming pool*.

3   **Manner** (*how* something happens):

She sings *beautifully*.

The children listened *intently*.

Gradually, the room filled with smoke.

4   **Reason** (*why* something happens):

> They saved money *in order to buy a house.*

> Simon left his job *because he was bored.*

> The festival is scheduled for 21 June, *to coincide with the summer solstice.*

See, also, section **4.6**.

1.14   Vocatives

A **Vocative** is used to identify the person or persons to whom a sentence is addressed:

> *James,* your dinner is ready.

> Come inside, *children.*

> *Doctor,* I need a new prescription.

> The car was parked behind the building, *your Honour.*

> I'm sorry I'm late, *everyone.*

> *Ladies and gentlemen,* thank you for that warm welcome.

Like Adjuncts (see section **1.12**), Vocatives are optional elements in sentence structure.

1.15   Sentence types

There are four major sentence types: declarative (see section **1.15.1**), interrogative (see section **1.15.2**), imperative (see section **1.15.3**) and exclamative (see section **1.15.4**).

1.15.1 *Declarative sentences*

A **declarative sentence** is typically used to convey information or to make a statement:

> This is Gladstone Park.

> David is listening to music.

Simon bought a new house.

James retired in 2006.

In a declarative sentence, the Subject usually comes first, and it is followed by the verb. Declarative sentences are by far the most common type.

1.15.2 Interrogative sentences

An **interrogative sentence** is used in asking a question and in seeking information:

Is this Gladstone Park?

Have you found a job yet?

Did you receive my email?

Do you take sugar?

Specifically, these are called *yes–no* **interrogatives**, because they expect either *yes* or *no* as the response.

Alternative interrogatives offer two or more alternative responses:

Do you want tea or coffee?

Is that a Picasso or a Dali?

Wh-**interrogatives** are introduced by a word beginning with *wh*, and they expect an open-ended response:

What are you reading?

Where do you work?

Who won the FA Cup in 2006?

The word *how* may also introduce an interrogative that expects an open-ended response:

How do you forward an email?

How can I get to Charing Cross?

How is your mother?

1.15.3 *Imperative sentences*

An **imperative sentence** is used to issue orders or instructions:

Wait a minute.

Take the overnight train from King's Cross.

Release the handbrake.

Cut the meat into cubes.

Imperative sentences usually have no Subject, as in these examples. However, the Subject *you* may sometimes be included for emphasis:

Don't *you* believe it.

You fix it (if you're so clever).

1.15.4 *Exclamative sentences*

Exclamative sentences are exclamations, and they are introduced by *what* or *how*:

What a fool I've been!

What a lovely garden you have!

How true that is!

How big you've grown!

In exclamative sentences, *what* is used to introduce noun phrases (see section 3.2), while *how* introduces all other types.

The four sentence types – declarative, interrogative, imperative and exclamative – have different grammatical forms. However, there is no one-to-one relationship between the form of a sentence and its role in communication. For instance, the following sentence has a declarative form:

You need more money.

However, if this is spoken with a rising intonation, it becomes a question:

You need more money?

Conversely, rhetorical questions have the form of an interrogative sentence, but they are really statements:

> What could be better than a day in London? (= 'Nothing could be better . . .')

> Who knows what the future will bring? (= 'Nobody knows . . .')

1.16 Fragments and non-sentences

All the sentences we have looked at so far have been grammatically complete. Grammatically complete sentences typically contain at least a Subject and a verb. However, a great deal of communication, especially in speech, consists of incomplete sentences or **fragments**. In conversation, for instance, speakers often omit the Subject, especially when the understood Subject is *I*:

> Must set my alarm clock tonight.

> Can't seem to concentrate today.

> Sounds lovely.

Fragments are also commonly used in response to questions:

> Speaker A: What did you buy for Sandra?

> Speaker B: *A gold necklace.*

Speaker B's utterance is a fragment, which we interpret in the same way as the complete sentence *I bought a gold necklace for Sandra.*

Newspaper headlines are often highly compressed, so that complete sentences are reduced to fragments:

LABOUR PARTY IN EXPENSES SCANDAL

This fragment has no verb, but we interpret it as the complete sentence *The Labour Party is involved in an expenses scandal.*

We refer to these as fragments because we can interpret them in the same way as grammatically complete sentences. Only some of the sentence elements are missing.

Non-sentences have no sentence structure at all, and they generally occur without any surrounding context. They are frequently used in public signs and notices:

No Parking

Motorway Ahead

Paddington, 2 miles

10% Off

Non-sentences in conversational English include *bye, goodbye, hello, no, ok, right, sure, thanks, thanks very much, yes*, as well as the interjections *ouch!, wow!, phew!, yippee!, yuk!*.

Fragments and non-sentences are a major feature of informal spoken English. In fact, they account for about one-third of all utterances in conversation.

Exercises

Exercise 1.1 Identifying the Subject (section 1.3)

In each of the following sentences, underline the Subject:

1 My eldest son graduated in June.
2 The students visited Paris with their teachers.
3 Some flights are very cheap.
4 The concert was very disappointing.
5 At Christmas, most of the children perform in the Nativity Play.
6 It's snowing.
7 It was in June that we met.
8 A year later, Tom and Amy were married.

Exercise 1.2 Identifying the Subject (section 1.3)

Rewrite each of the sentences below as questions (interrogatives), and underline the Subject in the question:

1 Paul is older than Amy.
2 Lunch is ready.
3 It is cold outside.
4 Someone is watching the house.
5 Alan has a new car.
6 Reading books is his favourite pastime.
7 It was Tom who made the suggestion.
8 His Facebook account is closed.

Exercise 1.3 Direct Object (section 1.6)

In each of the sentences below, underline the Direct Object.

1 The government has promised an end to age discrimination in the workplace.
2 Most people welcomed the government's change of policy.
3 However, some people expressed doubts about the proposed legislation.
4 They are demanding a more comprehensive review of employment law.
5 A Select Committee will discuss the issue next month.
6 The Committee is still accepting submissions.
7 Some people question the need for such extensive consultation.
8 The Opposition will raise the question during the next parliamentary session.

Exercise 1.4 Indirect Object (section 1.7)

Underline the Indirect Object in each of the sentences below.

1 Send me your email address, please.
2 He owes the bank a lot of money.
3 We've promised Paul a laptop for his birthday.
4 Can you tell us the way to King's Cross?
5 He is teaching the children French.
6 I've emailed you my details.
7 She gave the bridegroom a kiss.
8 They made both candidates the same offer.

Exercise 1.5 Direct Object (section 1.6) and Indirect Object (section 1.7)

Use each of the verbs below to make a sentence containing a Direct Object and an Indirect Object.

give	*pay*	*ask*	*find*	*charge*	*cook*	*show*
read	*tell*	*offer*	*cost*			

Exercise 1.6 Object Complement (section 1.8)

Underline the Object Complement in each of the sentences below.

1 Seafood can sometimes make people ill.
2 I usually find science fiction movies very boring.
3 They have named the baby Apple.
4 He proclaimed himself President of the new republic.
5 In 2006, *Time* magazine named him Person of the Year.
6 The alcohol made him drowsy.
7 He was appointed Chief Justice in 2008.
8 He calls himself the king of the jungle.

Exercise 1.7 The six sentence patterns (section 1.10) and Adjuncts (section 1.12)

In the spaces provided, indicate the function of each underlined element in the following sentences. Use the following abbreviations:

A = Adjunct   AC = Adverbial Complement
DO = Direct Object   IO = Indirect Object
S = Subject   SC = Subject Complement
OC = Object Complement

1 In tropical rainforests (   ), bird life (   ) is usually (   ) very exotic and colourful (   ).
2 The appearance of birds (   ) is seasonal (   ).
3 Sometimes (   ), the arrival of flowers and fruits (   ) will attract birds (   ).
4 The dense canopy of leaves (   ) makes the rainforest (   ) very dark (   ).
5 At ground level (   ), you (   ) can occasionally (   ) see kingfishers (   ).
6 The constant gloom and enormous tree trunks (   ) give the rainforest (   ) the appearance of a cathedral (   ).
7 The forest stretches three hundred miles eastwards (   ).

Exercise 1.8 Adjuncts (section 1.12)

Underline all the Adjuncts in the following passage.

RMS Titanic left Southampton on 10 April 1912. After crossing the English Channel, she stopped at Cherbourg, France. The next day, she stopped again at Queenstown, Ireland, to allow more passengers to go on board. When she finally sailed to New York, she had 2,240 passengers. On 14 April, just before midnight, the *Titanic* struck an iceberg in the north Atlantic. The massive ship sank two hours and forty minutes later. As a result, 1,517 people lost their lives. Unfortunately, the owners of the Titanic thought their ship was unsinkable. While they were fitting out the great ship, they did not provide enough lifeboats. Following the sinking, new regulations were introduced, in an effort to ensure that such a catastrophe could never happen again.

Chapter 2

Words and word classes

2.1   Open and closed word classes

Words may be divided into the following major word classes:

Word class	Examples
Nouns	brother, child, China, ecology, James, tree
Main verbs	break, consider, destroy, eat, sing, talk
Adjectives	angry, cold, foolish, happy, tidy, young
Adverbs	carefully, gradually, happily, slowly
Pronouns	I, me, my, you, he, his, her, we, our
Auxiliary verbs	can, could, do, may, might, will, would
Prepositions	after, at, for, in, of, over, with, without
Conjunctions	although, and, because, but, or, when
Articles	a, an, the
Numerals	one, two, twenty, first, second, third

Some word classes are **open**; that is, they admit new words as members as the need arises. The major open classes are the first two above – nouns and main verbs. The class of nouns is potentially infinite, as it is continually being expanded as new discoveries are made, new products are developed, and new ideas are explored. In recent years, for example, developments in Internet technology have given rise to many new nouns, including:

bitmap	browser
blog	cache
broadband	chatroom

e-commerce

firewall

gigabyte

homepage

hypertext

newsgroup

spam

voicemail

These developments have also given rise to some new verbs:

bookmark

double-click

download

reboot

right-click

surf

upload

The adjective and adverb classes also admit new members from time to time, though far less prolifically than the class of nouns. The class of numerals is entirely open, as we can always add 1 to a number to make a new number.

In contrast with this, prepositions, for instance, belong to a **closed word class**. We never invent new prepositions (words such as *after*, *at*, *before*, *in*, *with*), simply because we never need them.

2.2 Nouns

Nouns denote both concrete objects and abstract entities:

Concrete	Abstract
book	anger
chair	difficulty
dog	eagerness
grass	history
lake	information
house	progress
tree	terror

Many nouns can be identified by their characteristic endings:

-ence	absence, difference, evidence, experience
-ment	embarrassment, experiment, government, treatment
-tion	education, information, situation, vegetation
-ism	defeatism, optimism, symbolism, terrorism
-ist	artist, biologist, perfectionist, realist

For more examples of noun endings, see section 5.3.

2.2.1 │ Singular nouns and plural nouns

Most nouns have two forms, a **singular** form and a **plural** form. Regular nouns form the plural by adding *-s* to the singular:

Singular	Plural
boy	boys
table	tables

However, some very frequent nouns have irregular plurals:

Singular	Plural
man	men
woman	women
child	children
foot	feet
goose	geese
mouse	mice
tooth	teeth
sheep	sheep

The distinction between singular and plural is called **number contrast**.

For more on the spelling of plural nouns, see section **5.11**.

2.2.2 | Common nouns and proper nouns

Proper nouns are the names of individual people and places, including geographical features such as roads, rivers, mountains and oceans:

Patrick	Hong Kong
Nelson Mandela	Euston Road
China	Atlantic Ocean
Paris	River Thames
New Delhi	Mount Everest

The names of institutions, newspapers, buildings and ships are also proper nouns:

The Wall Street Journal	London Underground
The Royal Albert Hall	Titanic
Harvard University	Mayflower
Millennium Dome	British Museum

Finally, proper nouns include the days of the week, the months of the year and other periods of the calendar:

Monday	Christmas
Tuesday	Passover
January	Ramadan
February	Thanksgiving

Proper nouns are written with an initial capital (upper-case) letter. All other nouns are **common** nouns. As proper nouns usually refer to unique individuals, places or events in the calendar, they do not normally have a plural form. However, they may take a plural ending when number is specifically being referred to:

There are two *Patricks* in my class.

We first met two *Christmases* ago.

2.2.3 | Countable nouns and uncountable nouns

Singular nouns denote just one instance, while plural nouns denote more than one instance:

Singular	Plural
one boy	two boys, three boys, four boys . . .
one day	two days, three days, four days . . .
one computer	two computers, three computers, four computers . . .

These nouns are called **countable nouns**. In contrast, some nouns cannot be counted in this way:

*one advice, two advices, three advices . . .

*one furniture, two furnitures, three furnitures . . .

*one software, two softwares, three softwares . . .

These nouns are called **uncountable nouns**. Uncountable nouns refer to things that are considered as indivisible wholes, and therefore cannot be counted.

Uncountable nouns have two important grammatical features:

1 They have a singular form (*advice, furniture, software*), but no plural form (**advices, *furnitures, *softwares*).
2 They do not take *a* or *an* before them (**an advice, *a furniture, *a software*).

Other uncountable nouns include: fun, information, health, honesty, luck, luggage, mud, music, traffic.

Some nouns may be uncountable or countable, depending on how their meaning is perceived in a particular context. For example:

Do you take *sugar*?

Here, *sugar* is uncountable, since (a) it has no plural form (**Do you take sugars?*) and (b) it will not take *a* (**Do you take a sugar?*). On the other hand, *sugar* is countable in the following:

I take two *sugars*. (= 'two spoonfuls of sugar')

2.2.4 Genitive nouns

The **genitive** (sometimes called genitive case) is formed by adding 's (apostrophe s) to the singular form of a noun:

John's car

the baby's toys

the government's decision

my wife's sister

If the noun already has an -s ending because it is plural, we add the apostrophe alone to form the genitive:

the Farmers	the Farmers' Union
two doctors	two doctors' reports

With irregular plural nouns (see **2.2.1**), the genitive is formed by adding apostrophe s, just as above:

the children	the children's clothes
the men	the men's toiletries
the women	the women's group
the people	the people's decision

Nouns ending in -s, in which the -s does not denote a plural, generally take an apostrophe alone:

Prince Charles	Prince Charles' children
Martin Nichols	Martin Nichols' house

However, apostrophe s is also sometimes added:

Prince Charles's children

The genitive form of a noun expresses a very wide range of meanings. We exemplify the major meanings below:

1 possession: the baby's toys ('the toys belonging to the baby')
2 relationship: my wife's sister ('the sister of my wife')
3 general attribute: my son's age ('the age of my son')
4 subjective genitive: the government's decision ('the government made the decision')

5 objective genitive: the prisoner's release ('the authorities released the prisoner')

2.2.5 | Dependent genitives and independent genitives

Genitives are either dependent or independent. A **dependent** genitive is followed by a noun:

the *baby's* toys

a *student's* essay

Caroline's friend

An **independent** genitive is not followed by a noun:

a friend of *Caroline's*

a colleague of *Frank's*

an old army pal of *Jim's*

An independent genitive is often used in referring to relationships between people, as in these examples. Notice that this construction has a very specific meaning. The independent genitive *a friend of Caroline's* does not mean the same as the dependent genitive *Caroline's friend*:

Independent: We met a friend of Caroline's in Spain.

Dependent: We met Caroline's friend in Spain.

The independent genitive means 'one of Caroline's friends', who may or may not be known to the hearer. In contrast, the dependent genitive means 'one specific friend', who is assumed to be known to the hearer.

Independent genitives are also used in references to places and businesses:

She stayed at *Rebecca's*   = Rebecca's house

I ran into Jim in *Sainsbury's*   = Sainsbury's supermarket

I left my wallet in the *barber's*   = the barber's shop

See also **Possessive pronouns**, section **2.6.2**.

The gender of nouns

The **gender** of nouns plays an important role in the grammar of some languages. In French, for instance, a masculine noun, such as *ciel* (sky), requires the masculine form (*le*) of the definite article (*le ciel* = the sky). A feminine noun, such as *mer* (sea), requires the feminine form (*la*) of the definite article (*la mer* = the sea).

In English, however, nouns are not in themselves either masculine or feminine. They do not have grammatical gender, though they may refer to male or female people or animals:

The *waiter* was very efficient.   The *waitress* was very efficient.

The *tiger* roars at night.   The *tigress* roars at night.

These spelling differences (*waiter/waitress*, *tiger/tigress*) reflect distinctions of sex, but they have no grammatical implications. We use the same definite article *the*, whether we are referring to *the waiter* or *the waitress*, *the tiger* or *the tigress*.

Similarly, the natural distinctions reflected in such pairs as *brother/sister*, *father/mother* and *king/queen* have no implications for grammar. While they refer to specific sexes, these words are not masculine or feminine in themselves.

However, gender is important in English when we replace a noun with a **pronoun** (see **2.6**):

The *waiter* was very efficient.   ~*He* was very efficient.

The *waitress* was very efficient.   ~*She* was very efficient.

Here, the choice of pronoun (*he* or *she*) is determined by the sex of the person being referred to. Gender differences are also seen in other pronoun pairs, including *his/her* and *himself/herself*.

See also **Gender-neutral pronouns**, section **2.6.4**.

2.3   Main verbs

Main verbs include:

believe   read

break   see

destroy	run	
eat	sleep	
go	teach	
love	walk	
meet	work	

We distinguish them here from the **auxiliary verbs** (see section **2.7**), such as *can, could, may, might, must, shall, should, will, would*. Main verbs can occur as the *only* verb in a sentence:

Caroline *eats* pizza.

In contrast, an auxiliary verb such as *will* cannot occur alone:

*Caroline *will* pizza.

Instead, an auxiliary verb always occurs with a main verb:

Caroline *will eat* pizza.

2.3.1 | The five verb forms

Verbs have five forms:

1 the base form: Amy decided to *walk* to school.
2 the *-s* form: Amy *walks* to school.
3 the past form: Amy *walked* to school.
4 the *-ed* form: Amy has *walked* to school.
5 the *-ing* form: Amy is *walking* to school.

The endings *-s*, *-ed* and *-ing* are called **inflections** (see section **5.8**). The inflections are added to the **base form** of the verb.

In regular verbs, two of the forms are identical: the past form (*walked*) and the *-ed* form (*walked*). However, we must distinguish between these two forms, because they are not always identical. For example, the irregular verb *write* has the following five forms:

1 the base form: Amy loves to *write* poetry.
2 the *-s* form: Amy *writes* poetry.
3 the past form: Amy *wrote* a poem.
4 the *-ed* form: Amy has *written* a poem.
5 the *-ing* form: Amy is *writing* a poem.

See the Appendix for a list of irregular verbs, together with their five forms.

In the following sections, we look at each of the five verb forms in turn.

2.3.2 | *The base form*

The base form of a verb is the form that is listed in dictionaries, e.g., *eat*, *walk*, *talk*, *run*. The base form of a verb is used:

1   after *to*:

> We decided to *walk*.
>
> Amy loves to *write* poetry.

The combination of *to* and the base form of a verb is called the **infinitive**.

2   in the present tense, with all Subjects except *he*, *she* or *it* (the third person singular pronouns – see section **2.6.1**):

> I *walk*   we *walk*
>
> you *walk*   they *walk*

Compare:

he/she/it *walks* (= the -*s* form – see section **2.3.3**)

3   in imperative sentences (see section **1.15.3**):

> *Walk* quickly.
>
> Don't *move*.
>
> *Leave* your coat here.

4   in the subjunctive (see section **3.3.6**):

> I demand that she *resign* immediately.

2.3.3 | *The -s form*

The -*s* form of a verb is produced by adding -*s* to the base form. It is used only in the present tense, when the Subject of the verb is third person singular (see section **2.6.1**):

She *walks* to school.

Amy *writes* poetry.

Compare:

I *walk* to school. (= the base form, see section **2.3.2**)

2.3.4 | *The past form*

The past form of a verb is produced by adding *-ed* to the base form. It is used for the past tense, with all Subjects:

I *cooked* dinner last night.

You *cooked* dinner last night.

David *cooked* dinner last night.

We *cooked* dinner last night.

The children *cooked* dinner last night.

Irregular verbs form the past in a variety of ways:

They *caught* the train at 8 a.m.

She *took* a bus to the city centre.

They *left* at 12.

See the Appendix for a list of irregular verbs, together with their five forms.

2.3.5 | *The -ed form*

The term '*-ed* form' is just a convenient cover term. In fact, only regular verbs actually end in *-ed* in this form (e.g. *was destroyed*). Irregular verbs display a very wide variety of endings in the *-ed* form (e.g. *begun, brought, shown, stolen, written*). The *-ed* form is used:

1   after the passive auxiliary *be* (see section **2.7.3**):

The movie was *directed* by Quentin Tarantino.

The Queen was *shown* to her seat.

Our suitcases were *stolen* from the hotel.

Two new scenes were *written* for the final version.

2   after the perfective auxiliary *have* (see section **2.7.5**):

Quentin Tarantino has *directed* many movies.

The Mayor has *shown* the Queen to her seat.

Someone had *stolen* our suitcases.

The scriptwriter had *written* two new scenes.

3   in subordinate clauses (see section **4.1**):

Published in 2008, the book became a best-seller.

Stolen last year, the painting was recovered by police in Amsterdam.

See the Appendix for a list of irregular verb forms.

2.3.6 │ The -ing form

The *-ing* form of a verb is produced by adding *-ing* to the base form. This applies whether the verb is regular or irregular. The *-ing* form is used:

1   after the progressive auxiliary *be* (see section **2.7.4**):

She is *walking* to school.

Alan was *sleeping* when I arrived.

2   in subordinate clauses (see section **4.1**):

Paul slammed the door, *bringing* the ceiling down.

2.3.7 │ Irregular verbs

Many of the most common verbs in English are **irregular**. This means that their past form and their *-ed* form are not produced in the usual way (that is, by adding *-ed* to the base form). For instance, the verbs *bring*, *choose* and *think* are irregular:

Base	-s	Past	-ed	-ing
bring	brings	brought	brought	bringing
choose	chooses	chose	chosen	choosing
think	thinks	thought	thought	thinking

The irregular verbs display a great diversity of spelling in the past form and in the -ed form (see the Appendix). However, we can distinguish the following major groups:

1   The base form ends in d, and the past form and the -ed form end in t:

Base	-s	Past	-ed	-ing
bend	bends	bent	bent	bending
build	builds	built	built	building
send	sends	sent	sent	sending
spend	spends	spent	spent	spending

2   The base form has i, the past form has a, and the -ed form has u:

Base	-s	Past	-ed	-ing
begin	begins	began	begun	beginning
drink	drinks	drank	drunk	drinking
sing	sings	sang	sung	singing
swim	swims	swam	swum	swimming

3   The base form has ee or ea, and the past form and the -ed form have e:

Base	-s	Past	-ed	-ing
bleed	bleeds	bled	bled	bleeding
feed	feeds	fed	fed	feeding
keep	keeps	kept	kept	keeping
leave	leaves	left	left	leaving

4   The base form is identical to the past form and the *-ed* form:

Base	-s	Past	-ed	-ing
cut	cuts	*cut*	*cut*	cutting
hit	hits	*hit*	*hit*	hitting
put	puts	*put*	*put*	putting
quit	quits	*quit*	*quit*	quitting

5   The past form and the *-ed* form are identical, and end in *-ought* or *-aught*:

Base	-s	Past	-ed	-ing
bring	brings	*brought*	*brought*	bringing
buy	buys	*bought*	*bought*	buying
catch	catches	*caught*	*caught*	catching
teach	teaches	*taught*	*taught*	teaching

2.3.8 | *Regular and irregular variants*

Some irregular verbs have regular variants that may be used for both the past form and the *-ed* form. In the following examples, both the regular *dreamed* and the irregular *dreamt* are used as the past form:

Regular: She *dreamed* she was on a hill overlooking the sea.

Irregular: I can't remember what I *dreamt* last night.

Similarly, the two variants *learned* and *learnt* are used as the *-ed* form in these examples:

Regular: The government ought to have *learned* from the economic downturn.

Irregular: Some governments have *learnt* valuable lessons from the recession.

The following verbs also have regular and irregular variants:

burn	burned/*burnt*	dive	dived/*dove*
knit	knitted/*knit*	lean	leaned/*leant*

leap	leaped/*leapt*	prove	proved/*proven*
smell	smelled/*smelt*	spell	spelled/*spelt*
spill	spilled/*spilt*	spoil	spoiled/*spoilt*

In general, American English tends to prefer the regular variants (e.g. *I dreamed last night* rather than *I dreamt last night*).

2.3.9 | **The verb be**

The verb *be* is very irregular and exhibits a total of eight different forms. These forms are shown here:

Base form	Present-tense forms	Past-tense forms	-*ed* form	-*ing* form
be	I *am*	I *was*	been	being
	you *are*	you *were*		
	he/she/it *is*	he/she/it *was*		
	we *are*	we *were*		
	you *are*	you *were*		
	they *are*	they *were*		

Many of these forms are contracted in informal use:

I	`m	= *am*
he/she/it	`s	= *is*
you/we/they	`re	= *are*

Some of the forms also have contracted negative counterparts:

he/she/it	*isn't*	= *is not*
he/she/it	*wasn't*	= *was not*
you/we/they	*aren't*	= *are not*
you/we/they	*weren't*	= *were not*

In British English, the form *aren't* is used as a contraction of *am not* in tag questions (see section **4.7.3**):

I am right about that, *aren't I?*

2.3.10 *Multi-word verbs*

Multi-word verbs are combinations of a verb and one or more other words. The combinations function like a single verb. We distinguish three types:

1 **Phrasal verbs** are combinations of a verb and an adverb (see section **2.5**):

The music *faded away* as we left the station.

The engine *cut out* just before landing.

Weigh up all the factors before making a decision.

Jeremy has been *trying out* the car in the Alps.

2 **Prepositional verbs** are combinations of a verb and a preposition (see section **2.8**):

I'll *look into* the matter immediately.

Amy doesn't *approve of* smoking.

The barrister *called for* a unanimous verdict.

Paul is *looking after* his sister.

3 **Phrasal-prepositional verbs** are combinations of a verb, an adverb and a preposition:

I won't *put up with* this noise any longer.

I *went along with* their ideas for the sake of peace.

Members of the Huntu tribe *shy away from* violence.

Don't *give in to* his demands.

2.4 Adjectives

Adjectives express a quality or attribute of a noun:

a *happy* child	a *surly* person	*toxic* waste
an *old* man	*defective* brakes	a *greedy* child
a *red* flag	a *dangerous* road	a *large* hotel

In certain uses, the attribute is not directly related to the noun itself, and the adjective must be interpreted in a different way. Compare the following pairs:

an *old* car ('a car that is old')	an *old* schoolmate ('a former schoolmate')
a *small* man ('a man who is small')	a *small* businessman ('a man with a small business')
a *heavy* suitcase ('a suitcase that is heavy')	a *heavy* drinker ('someone who drinks heavily')

Typical adjective endings include:

-al   biological, classical, clinical, environmental, theatrical

-ble   accessible, comfortable, possible, responsible, terrible

-ive   constructive, deceptive, defective, furtive, interactive

-ous   continuous, delicious, enormous, rigorous, serious

-y   funny, greedy, happy, rainy, tasty, weary

Most adjectives can occur before a noun (the **attributive** position), or after a linking verb (the **predicative** position) (see section **1.4.2**):

a *violent* storm   ~the storm was *violent*

a *delicious* meal   ~the meal is *delicious*

However, a small number of adjectives are restricted to just one position. The adjective *afraid*, for instance, can only appear in the predicative position:

the children were *afraid*   *~the *afraid* children

Conversely, the adjective *chief* can only appear in the attributive position:

the *chief* result   *~ the result is *chief*

In a small number of fixed expressions, an adjective appears immediately after the noun (the **postpositive** position):

the people *responsible*

the Princess *Royal*

the heir *apparent*

the roadway *proper*

Adjectives can also modify a small number of pronouns (see section **2.6**). They always follow the pronoun:

something *terrible*

someone *new*

nobody *special*

nothing *unusual*

2.4.1 | *Gradable adjectives*

Most adjectives can take a modifying word, such as *fairly*, *very* or *extremely*, before them:

fairly *cold*   very *cold*   extremely *cold*

The modifying word locates the adjective on a relative scale of intensity. In this example, the scale is from *fairly cold* to *extremely cold*. This characteristic of adjectives is called **gradability**.

The modifying words (*fairly*, *very*, *extremely*) are called **intensifiers** (see section **2.5.3**).

2.4.2 | *Comparative adjectives and superlative adjectives*

The adjective *cold* has two other forms, *colder* (the **comparative form**) and *coldest* (the **superlative form**). The form *cold* is called the base form. Most adjectives have these three forms. Here are some more examples:

Base form	Comparative form	Superlative form
new	newer	newest
old	older	oldest
dark	darker	darkest
big	bigger	biggest

The comparative form is produced by adding an *-er* ending to the base form. The superlative form is produced by adding an *-est* ending, again to the base:

Base *cold*   + *-er*   = comparative *colder*

Base *cold*   + *-est*   = superlative *coldest*

Some adjectives form the comparative and superlative using *more* and *most*, respectively:

Base form	Comparative form	Superlative form
recent	more recent	most recent
important	more important	most important

In general, adjectives with one syllable in the base form take the *-er* and *-est* endings, while longer words use *more* and *most*:

Base form	Comparative form	Superlative form
warm	warmer	warmest
hopeful	more hopeful	most hopeful
beautiful	more beautiful	most beautiful
complicated	more complicated	most complicated

The adjectives *good* and *bad* have irregular comparative and superlative forms:

Base form	Comparative form	Superlative form
good	better	best
bad	worse	worst

2.4.3 | Participial adjectives

Participial adjectives have the endings *-ed* or *-ing* that we normally associate with verbs (see section **2.3.1**):

a *complicated* process	an *amazing* achievement
a *crazed* expression	a *boring* book
a *disabled* person	a *confusing* account
an *embarrassed* smile	a *fascinating* photograph
an *experienced* driver	a *rewarding* experience
a *talented* singer	a *disappointing* result

Most participial adjectives have a corresponding verb (*to complicate*, *to amaze*, etc), but some do not. For example, there is no verb **to talent*, corresponding to *a talented singer*.

Like other adjectives, participial adjectives may be gradable:

> a very complicated process

> an extremely disappointing result

They also have comparative and superlative forms:

complicated	more complicated	most complicated
disappointing	more disappointing	most disappointing

See also **Adjective phrases**, section **3.4**.

2.5   Adverbs

Many adverbs are formed by adding *-ly* to an adjective (see section **2.4**):

Adjective	Adverb
certain	certainly
extreme	extremely
exact	exactly
mad	madly
quick	quickly
slow	slowly
soft	softly

However, by no means all adverbs end in *-ly*. In particular, many adverbs referring to time and place have no distinctive ending. These include:

afterwards	now
away	soon
back	there
here	today
inside	tomorrow
never	yesterday

Note also that some adjectives end in *-ly*, including *costly, deadly, friendly, kindly, lively* and *timely*.

The words *hard* and *fast* can be used as both adverbs and adjectives:

Adverb: John works *hard*.
Peter drives *fast*.

Adjective: John is used to *hard* work.
Peter drives a *fast* car.

Adverbs are most commonly used to modify:

1 a verb:

Amy speaks *softly*.

David works *quickly*.

Paul will arrive *soon*.

2 an adjective:

really slow

terribly warm

extremely rude

3 another adverb:

fairly slowly

very closely

extremely badly

For more about adding *-ly* to adjectives, see section **5.10**.

| 2.5.1 | *Gradable adverbs* |

Many adverbs are gradable; that is, they can take a modifying word, such as *fairly* or *very*, which locates the adverb on a scale of intensity:

fairly slowly	*very* slowly	*extremely* slowly
fairly suddenly	*very* suddenly	*extremely* suddenly

2.5.2 | Comparative adverbs and superlative adverbs

Some adverbs exhibit three forms: the base form, the comparative form (ending in -*er*) and the superlative form (ending in -*est*):

Base form	Comparative form	Superlative form
John works *hard*.	Mary works *harder*.	Paul work *hardest*.
John drives *fast*.	Mary drives *faster*.	Paul drives *fastest*.

However, most adverbs express comparison using the words *more* and *most*:

Base form	Comparative form	Superlative form
importantly	more importantly	most importantly
probably	more probably	most probably
recently	more recently	most recently

2.5.3 | Intensifiers

An **intensifier** is a special type of adverb that is used to express intensity in an adjective or in another adverb. The most common intensifier is *very*:

very cold   *very* suddenly

very eager   *very* soon

Other intensifiers include *almost, completely, entirely, extremely, fairly, highly, quite, slightly, totally, utterly*.

In informal use, and especially in spoken English, the word *pretty* is often used as an intensifier:

The weather was *pretty* bad.

I'm *pretty* sure we'll be late.

You'll have to move *pretty* quickly.

I'll be there *pretty* soon.

2.5.4 | *The meanings of adverbs*

Adverbs express three major types of meaning:

1 **Manner** adverbs indicate *how* something happens:

> The child was playing *happily* in the garden.
>
> Paul writes *beautifully*.
>
> The thief crept *silently* along the roof.
>
> The passengers waited *calmly* for the lifeboats.

Other manner adverbs include *carefully*, *clearly*, *dangerously*, *heavily*, *heroically*, *patiently*, *quietly*, *quickly*, *rapidly*, *scientifically*, *slowly*, *softly* and *spontaneously*.

2 **Time** adverbs indicate *when* something happened, as well as frequency of occurrence:

> We visited Rome *recently*.
>
> Bernard has an interview *tomorrow*.
>
> I'm hoping to retire *soon*.
>
> *Sometimes* we go to Joe's in the High Street.

Other time adverbs include: *afterwards*, *again*, *always*, *never*, *now*, *often*, *presently*, *previously*, *rarely*, *then*, *today* and *yesterday*.

3 **Place** adverbs indicate a *place* or a *direction*:

> Leave your coat *there*.
>
> Why are you still *here*?
>
> She just turned and walked *away*.
>
> The car shot *forward* when I released the clutch.

Other place adverbs include: *backwards*, *downwards*, *everywhere*, *inside*, *outside* and *somewhere*.

See also **Adverb phrases**, section **3.5**.

2.6 Pronouns

Many pronouns can be used as substitutes for nouns:

David loves football. *He* supports Manchester United.

Here, the pronoun *he* substitutes for the noun *David*, to which it refers back. Using the pronoun means that we can avoid repeating the noun.

The major subclasses of pronouns are:

Personal pronouns :   *I/me, he/him* etc.   (see section **2.6.1**)

Possessive pronouns: *my/mine, your/yours* etc. (see section **2.6.2**)

Reflexive pronouns: *myself, yourself* etc.   (see section **2.6.3**)

As Table 2.1 shows, these three subclasses are closely related to each other. We discuss each subclass in the following sections.

Table 2.1 Personal, possessive, and reflexive pronouns

Person	Number	Gender	Personal pronouns		Possessive pronouns		Reflexive pronouns
			Subjective	Objective	Dependent	Independent	
1st	Singular	–	I	me	my	mine	myself
2nd	Singular	–	you	you	your	yours	yourself
3rd	Singular	Masculine	he	him	his	his	himself
		Feminine	she	her	her	hers	herself
		Non-personal	it	it	its	–	itself
1st	Plural	–	we	us	our	ours	ourselves
2nd	Plural	–	you	you	your	yours	yourselves
3rd	Plural	–	they	them	their	theirs	themselves

2.6.1 | *Personal pronouns*

The **personal pronouns** (see Table 2.1) exhibit contrasts for **person** (first person, second person or third person), **number** (singular or plural) and **case** (subjective or objective). In addition, the third person singular pronouns *he/she/it* exhibit a contrast for **gender** (masculine, feminine or non-personal).

The **subjective** forms of the personal pronouns are used when the pronoun is the Subject of the sentence (see section **1.2**):

I gave David a present.

You need a holiday, Sam.

He/she/it needs medical help.

We travelled by plane.

You should all complete an application form.

They enjoyed the film.

The **objective** forms are used in all other positions. These positions are:

1   after a verb (see section **2.3**):

David gave *me* a present.

I'll see *you* soon.

The minister supports *him/her/it*.

Marie met *us* at the airport.

I'll bring *you* a nice surprise.

Susan telephoned *them*.

2   after a preposition (see section **2.8**):

David gave it to *me*.

I'll probably get there before *you*.

She arrived after *him/her/it*.

He's not coming with *us*.

I'm tired talking to *you* people.

I'm writing a song for *them*.

There is no formal distinction between subjective *you* and objective *you*:

Subjective: *You* emailed me yesterday.

Objective: I emailed *you* yesterday.

Likewise, there is no formal distinction between singular *you* and plural *you*. When necessary, speakers and writers make the reference explicitly plural by expanding it, for instance by using *both of you*, *you both*, *all of you*, *you people*, *you all*, *you guys* (American English, informal).

2.6.2 | *Possessive pronouns*

The **possessive pronouns** (see Table 2.1) exhibit contrasts for person (first person, second person or third person) and for number (singular or plural). Like the personal pronouns (see section **2.6.1**), possessive pronouns have gender-based contrasts (masculine, feminine or non-personal) in the third person singular.

Each possessive pronoun has two distinct forms, the dependent form and the independent form. **Dependent** possessives are used before a noun:

This is *my* car.

I've borrowed *your* computer.

She took *his/her/its* photograph.

We've lost *our* way.

They sold *their* house.

Independent possessives are used without a following noun. They most commonly occur after *of*, in independent genitives (see section **2.2.5**):

a friend of *mine*

this partner of *yours*

a colleague of *his/hers*

an uncle of *ours*

that dog of *yours*

a relative of *theirs*

Independent possessives also occur in other positions, especially when the context makes clear what the pronoun refers to:

John's car is fast, but *mine* is cheaper to run.
('mine' = 'my car')

You are in my address book, but am I in *yours*?
('yours' = 'your address book')

The non-personal possessive pronoun *its* cannot be used independently. Compare:

> The blue ribbon is *his*.
>
> The red ribbon is *hers*.
>
> *The yellow ribbon is *its*.

Its can only be used dependently, before a noun:

> The horse shook *its* head.

2.6.3 | Reflexive pronouns

The **reflexive pronouns** end in *-self* (singular) or *-selves* (plural) (see Table 2.1). They exhibit distinctions of person (first person, second person or third person) and number (singular or plural). The third person singular reflexives (*himself/herself/itself*) show distinctions of gender (masculine, feminine or non-personal).

The reflexive pronouns are used to refer back to the Subject of the same sentence:

> Michael was very badly injured and is now unable to feed *himself*.

Here, *himself* refers back to *Michael*, the Subject of the sentence.

Less commonly, reflexive pronouns are used for emphasis:

> The Chancellor mentioned tax cuts, but he *himself* knows that the time is not right for reform.

Here, the reflexive *himself* co-occurs with the corresponding personal pronoun (**subjective case**) *he*. Similarly:

I myself	we ourselves
you yourself	they themselves
she herself	

2.6.4 | Gender-neutral pronouns

English lacks a **gender-neutral pronoun** in the singular. *He* is masculine, and *she* is feminine, but no pronoun exists to refer to people of unknown or unidentified sex (*it* can only be used to refer to objects and animals, not to people). Therefore, a problem arises in sentences such as:

Somebody has left *his* coat behind.

Clearly, the sex of 'somebody' is not known, and so there is no way of knowing whether to use *his coat* or *her coat*. Traditionally, the masculine *his* has been used in these circumstances, as in the example above.

However, the arbitrary choice of *his* over *her* is now felt by many people to be unacceptably sexist. A common solution is to use *his or her* (or *his/her*):

Somebody has left *his or her* coat behind.

Likewise, the subjective pronouns *he or she*, *he/she* (and even *s/he*) are sometimes used as gender-neutral pronouns:

Encourage your child to read when *he or she* reaches the age of 3.

However, this can be stylistically irritating, especially when it is repeated:

He or she has to satisfy the jury that *he or she* is right.

A candidate who wishes to enter the school before *his or her* eighteenth birthday may be asked to write to state *his or her* reasons.

In recent years, the plural pronouns *their* (possessive) and *they* (subjective) are increasingly being used in these contexts as gender-neutral pronouns:

Somebody has left *their* coat behind.

Encourage your child to read when *they* reach the age of 3.

2.6.5 | *Demonstrative pronouns*

The **demonstrative pronouns** are:

this, that, these, those

This and *that* are singular and are used with singular nouns:

Do you need *this* pen?

I really like *that* plant.

These and *those* are plural and are used with plural nouns:

Who owns *these* pens?

We should buy some of *those* plants.

The demonstrative pronouns may also be used independently, that is, without a following noun:

This is a great film.

That is the challenge we face.

These are very good apples.

Those are quite cheap.

2.6.6 | *Relative pronouns*

The **relative pronouns** are:

who, whom, whose, which, that

Relative pronouns introduce a relative clause (see section **4.3.2**):

That's the man *who* lives beside us.

That's the man *whom* we met yesterday.

The problem *which* we're facing is very serious.

The thing *that* worries me most is the overdraft.

Who and *whom* differ in case. *Who* is subjective:

the man *who* lives beside us (cf. *the man* lives beside us)

while *whom* is objective:

the man *whom* we met (cf. we met *the man*)

In formal contexts, and especially in writing, *whom* is used after a preposition (see section **2.8**):

the person on *whom* we rely

the people with *whom* he used to work

the people to *whom* it is addressed

In less formal contexts, including everyday speech, *whom* is often omitted altogether, and the preposition is moved to the end:

the person we rely on

the people he used to work with

the people it is addressed to

Pronoun **it**

The pronoun *it* has two major uses:

1   As a personal pronoun (see section **2.6.1**), *it* can replace a third person singular noun with non-human reference:

> *The car* skidded on ice.   *It* skidded on ice.
>
> Paul left *his coat* at school.   ~Paul left *it* at school.

2   *It* is used in expressions relating to the weather and to time:

> *It* is very cold.
>
> *It* rained last night.
>
> *It* is four o'clock.
>
> *It* is getting late.

This is sometimes called 'empty *it*' or 'dummy *it*', because *it* does not refer to anything in particular. Empty *it* is also used, with even more vague reference, in many other expressions, including:

> Hold *it*! (= 'Stop')
>
> Take *it* easy!
>
> Can you make *it* to my party tonight?

See also **Cleft sentences** (section **4.17**) and **Postponed Subjects** (section **4.18**).

Pronoun **one**

The pronoun *one* has two distinct uses:

1   Substitute *one* is used as a substitute for a noun that has been mentioned earlier:

> The black coat is nice but I prefer the green *one*.

Here, the pronoun *one* substitutes for the noun *coat* (cf. *I prefer the green coat*). Further examples of substitute *one* include:

> The problem is a complex *one*.
> (*one* = 'problem')

The house was not a modern *one*, but it was comfortable. (*one* = 'house')

I need a scanner so I'll just have to buy *one*. (*one* = 'a scanner')

Substitute *one* has a plural form, *ones*:

The black coats are nice, but I prefer the green *ones*.

2 Generic *one* carries a generic meaning corresponding approximately to 'people in general':

One can't expect miracles.

One loses interest as *one* gets older.

Generic *one* has a genitive form, *one's*:

When one is cold, *one's* capillaries close to minimise heat loss.

The corresponding reflexive pronoun (see section **2.6.3**) is *oneself*:

One could easily find *oneself* out of a job.

Generic *one* is considered by many speakers to be quite formal. It can often be replaced by the less formal *you*:

You could easily find *yourself* out of a job.

2.7   Auxiliary verbs

In section 2.3, we introduced the distinction between a main verb, such as *believe, eat, love*, and an auxiliary verb, such as *can, may, might, will*. We said that a main verb can occur alone in a sentence:

Caroline *eats* pizza.

whereas an auxiliary verb such as *will* cannot occur alone:

*Caroline *will* pizza.

An auxiliary verb always occurs with a main verb:

Caroline *will eat* pizza.

Auxiliary verbs are sometimes called **helping verbs**, because they 'help' the main verb in some way. For instance, in *Caroline will eat pizza*, the auxiliary verb *will* expresses prediction.

The **modal auxiliary** verbs (or 'modals') are:

can	shall
could	should
may	will
might	would
must	

Here are examples of the modals in use:

We *can* visit the park if the weather is fine.

She *could* sense that something was wrong.

Susan *may* be late tomorrow morning.

I *might* see you again before I leave.

You *must* try a little harder.

I *shall* speak to him on his return.

David *should* join the army.

The play *will* open on 17 March.

I *would* love a game of tennis.

The modals have corresponding negative forms:

can	*can't/cannot*
could	*couldn't*
may	*mayn't* (British English – rare)
might	*mightn't*
must	*mustn't*
shall	*shan't* (British English – rare)
should	*shouldn't*
will	*won't*
would	*wouldn't*

Traditional grammars made a very sharp distinction between *shall* and *will*. They recommended that *shall* should be used to express future time with *I* as Subject ('I *shall* arrive at six'), and that *will* should be used with all other Subjects ('He *will* arrive at six.'). The reverse was recommended when expressing intention: 'I *will* work hard', but 'He *shall* work hard'.

In fact, these distinctions no longer apply in common use, if they ever did apply. The word *shall* has more or less disappeared from American English, and there is evidence that it is also in decline in British English, except perhaps in the most formal contexts. *Will* is the preferred form in both varieties.

2.7.2 | *The meanings of modal auxiliaries*

The modal auxiliary verbs express a very wide range of meanings. The principal meanings are:

- Permission:

    You *may* go in now.

    Can I have a piece of chocolate?

    Years ago, people *could* cross the border without a visa.

- Obligation:

    You *must* complete both sides of the form.

    Safety *should* be our top priority.

- Ability:

    David *can* play the guitar.

    My grandfather *could* dance the Charleston.

- Prediction:

    I *will* be home at seven.

    I *shall* write as soon as I can.

    We *won't* stay very long.

- Probability or Possibility:

    She *may* have gone home.

You *must* be very tired.

They *should* be home by now.
(= 'I assume that they are home by now')

Heavy snow *can* cause real problems for motorists.

2.7.3 | *The passive auxiliary* be

The **passive auxiliary** *be* is used to form a passive sentence (see section **1.11**):

- Passive:

    The play *was* written by Tom Stoppard.

Compare:

- Active:

    Tom Stoppard wrote the play.

The passive auxiliary is followed by the *-ed* form of a verb (see section **2.3.5**).

The verb *get* is sometimes used as a passive auxiliary:

It started to rain as I left the house, and I *got* soaked.

At the end of the film, the villain *gets* shot by the police.

2.7.4 | *The progressive auxiliary* be

As the name suggests, the **progressive auxiliary** *be* is used to denote action in progress:

Paul *is* learning French.

It also has a past form:

Paul *was* learning French.

The progressive auxiliary is followed by the *-ing* form of a verb (see section **2.3.6**).

See also **Aspect**, section **3.3.5**.

2.7.5 | *The perfective auxiliary* have

The **perfective auxiliary** is *have*:

Peter *has* injured his foot.

Caroline *has* finished her dissertation.

We *had* discussed the matter at an earlier meeting.

I *had* met Mr Callaghan before.

The perfective auxiliary is followed by the *-ed* form of a verb (see section 2.3.5).

See also **Aspect**, section **3.3.5**.

2.7.6 | *Auxiliary* do

The **auxiliary** verb *do* has three main uses:

1   in forming questions:

Do you like Robert?

Did you enjoy the match?

Does your father use a computer?

2   in forming negative statements, with *not*:

I *do* not want it.

She *did* not graduate.

Simon *does* not eat cheese.

3   in negative imperatives, with *not*:

Do not touch that.

Do not move.

In informal use, *do not* is often contracted to *don't*:

Don't touch that.

Don't move.

2.7.7 | Semi-auxiliaries

Semi-auxiliaries are Multi-word auxiliary verbs, including:

be about to	happen to	seem to
be going to	have to	tend to
be supposed to	mean to	used to

Like the other auxiliaries, semi-auxiliaries occur before a main verb:

The meeting *is about to* start.

David *is going to* retire at the end of August.

MPs *are supposed to* declare their financial interests.

Paul's car broke down so he *had to* walk.

Ottoman art *tends to* be very stylised.

2.8   Prepositions

The class of prepositions includes the following words:

about	below	in	to
across	between	into	toward(s)
after	by	of	under
against	down	off	until
at	during	on	up
before	for	over	with
behind	from	through	without

Prepositions are mainly used to introduce a noun phrase (see section **3.2**):

after dark	*for* the children
across the road	*from* London
after the war	*under* suspicion
around the world	*with* mayonnaise
before my lunch	*without* fear

In themselves, prepositions are essentially meaningless, but they combine with the noun phrase that follows them to create meaningful units, which are called **prepositional phrases** (see section **3.6**). The major meanings of these phrases can be summarised as follows (the prepositional phrases are underlined):

1 **space** (location/direction/relative position):

> We are travelling _to London_.
>
> He comes _from Australia_.
>
> We met Paul _at the station_.
>
> Amy found money _under the floorboards_.
>
> Put the mouse _on a mousepad_.
>
> The car skidded _across the motorway_.
>
> She leaned _against the door_.
>
> A river runs _through the valley_.

2 **time/duration**:

> We're leaving _at 2 p.m._
>
> He was born _in October 1991_.
>
> I'll visit the library _for a few hours_.
>
> We have an exam _on Wednesday_.
>
> He can't come _before the weekend_.

3 **cause/purpose**:

> He does it _for his children_.
>
> He died _of pneumonia_.
>
> He is suffering _from fatigue_.
>
> He succeeded _through hard work_.

4 **accompaniment**:

> The President arrived _with his entourage_.
>
> She won't go anywhere _without her mobile phone_.

5 concession:

> He never reads anything _except_ Stephen King novels.

> We had a good time, _despite the rain_.

Multi-word prepositions are two- and three-word combinations that act as a unit:

according to	in accordance with
ahead of	in front of
apart from	in relation to
because of	in spite of
by means of	in terms of
due to	on behalf of

See also **Prepositional phrases**, section **3.6**.

2.9   Conjunctions

Conjunctions are used to link phrases and clauses together. There are two types:

1   **coordinating conjunctions** (or simply 'coordinators') are used to link elements of _equal_ grammatical status. The main coordinators are _and_, _but_ and _or_:

> The weather was [cold] _and_ [wet].

> [Paul plays football] _and_ [Amy enjoys tennis].

> [Simon is coming] _but_ [he can't stay for long].

> [I read your book] _but_ [I didn't enjoy it].

> Would you prefer [coffee] _or_ [cappuccino]?

> [You can leave now] _or_ [you can wait here].

The coordinator _or_ is used with _either_:

> You can have _either_ [pizza] _or_ [a hamburger].

In the negative counterpart of this, the coordinator *nor* is used with *neither*:

You can have *neither* [pizza] *nor* [a hamburger].

On **coordination**, see section **4.8**.

2 **subordinating conjunctions** (or simply 'subordinators') introduce a subordinate clause:

Paul has to leave *because* he has a dental appointment.

Here, the **main clause** is *Paul has to leave*. The subordinate clause is *because he has a dental appointment*, and it is introduced by the subordinator *because*.

Other subordinators include:

although	that
after	unless
as	until
before	when(ever)
if	whereas
since	while

Multi-word subordinators include the following:

as long as	in order that
as soon as	provided that
as though	so long as
except that	such that

For more on subordinate clauses, see Chapter 4.

2.10 Articles

The **articles** are *the* and *a/an*. Articles always occur before a noun, and they express the kind of reference that the noun has.

The **definite article** *the* is used to express definite reference:

We saw *the* play in London.

This refers to 'a particular play', which must have been previously identified. Compare:

We saw *a* play in London.

This refers to 'some unspecified play', which may be identified later:

We saw *a* play in London. It was *The Chairs* by Eugène Ionesco.

The definite article *the* is also used to express **generic reference**, that is, to refer to a species or group as a whole:

The humpback whale is an endangered species.

The **indefinite article** is *a*, and its variant is *an*. The choice between these variants is determined by the initial sound (not the spelling) of the word that follows the article. *A* is used when the following word begins with a consonant sound:

a chair	*a* large salary
a film	*a* UFO
a huge increase	

An is used when the following word begins with a vowel sound:

an active person	*an* MA course
an eager student	*an* overture
an examination	*an* X-ray
an L-plate	*an* unexploded bomb

The indefinite article is only used with singular, countable nouns. The definite article *the* is used with singular and plural nouns:

	Singular	Plural
Countable	a castle	*a castles
	the castle	the castles
Uncountable	*a traffic	—
	the traffic	—

Uncountable nouns have no plural form – see section **2.2.3**.

2.11 Numerals

Numerals include all numbers, whether written as words (*one*, *two*, *three*) or as digits (*1*, *2*, *3*). There are two main subclasses of numerals:

1 **Cardinal numerals** refer to quantity:

zero, nought, 0	fifty, 50
one, 1	one hundred, 100
two, 2	one thousand, 1,000
three, 3	

2 **Ordinal numerals** refer to positions in an ordered sequence:

first, 1st	fiftieth, 50th
second, 2nd	one hundredth, 100th
third, 3rd	one thousandth, 1,000th

By analogy with *first*, the words *last* and *next* are also ordinal numerals, although they cannot be written as digits.

Exercises

Exercise 2.1 Nouns (section 2.2)

Convert the following words into nouns by adding noun endings and making any other necessary spelling changes. Some words may take more than one ending to form two or more different nouns.

argue	humiliate	refer
capitalise	improvise	require
compensate	intervene	specialise
criticise	occur	state
develop	offend	
disappoint	perceive	

69

Exercise 2.2 Singular nouns and plural nouns (section 2.2.1)

Supply the plural form of each of the singular nouns listed below:

analysis	hypothesis
basis	medium
bureau	phenomenon
crisis	sister-in-law
criterion	stimulus
formula	wolf

Exercise 2.3 The five verb forms (section 2.3.1)

Indicate the form of the underlined verb in each of the following sentences:

1 Everyone <u>understands</u> ( ) the need to <u>reduce</u> ( ) carbon emissions.
2 If you <u>care</u> ( ) about the environment, <u>take</u> ( ) action now.
3 One way we all <u>waste</u> ( ) resources is by <u>leaving</u> ( ) lights switched on at home when we're not even there.
4 Governments have only recently <u>realised</u> ( ) that carbon emissions <u>threaten</u> ( ) our future.
5 In the 1970s, environmental groups <u>tried</u> ( ) to <u>raise</u> ( ) our awareness of the problem.
6 They have <u>given</u> ( ) us a lot to <u>think</u> ( ) about.

Exercise 2.4 Irregular verbs (section 2.3.7)

Supply the correct form of the irregular verb in the following sentences:

1 I have . . . a wonderful book on astronomy. (find)
2 He may have . . . his partner. (tell)
3 The suspect was . . . to Paddington police station. (bring)
4 Large areas of the coastline were . . . away by the tsunami. (sweep)
5 I have been . . . to secrecy. (swear)
6 He . . . in cash for a brand-new Porsche. (pay)
7 It was . . . to be a surprise. (mean)
8 The castle had . . . empty for years. (lie)
9 The money was . . . into the lining of his jacket. (sew)
10 The animals were . . . to safety. (lead)

Exercise 2.5 Adjectives (section 2.4)

Convert the following words into adjectives by adding adjective endings and making any other necessary spelling changes. Some words may take more than one ending to form two or more different adjectives.

cure	glory	music	reason
disruption	legend	nausea	religion
drizzle	leak	periphery	tedium
geology	mass	question	wool

Exercise 2.6 Comparative adjectives and superlative adjectives (section 2.4.2)

Supply the comparative and superlative forms of each of the following adjectives:

brilliant	handsome
clever	lucky
elegant	warm
fast	wonderful

Exercise 2.7 Adverbs (section 2.5)

Convert the following adjectives to adverbs by adding -ly and making any other necessary spelling changes:

absolute	environmental	memorable
capable	happy	personal
clear	lazy	terrible
demonstrable	legal	
dull	lucky	

Exercise 2.8 The meanings of adverbs (section 2.5.4)

In each of the following sentences, indicate the kind of meaning that is expressed by the underlined adverbs. Use the following abbreviations:

M = manner   P = place   T = time

1   The choir sang <u>beautifully</u> ( ).
2   We'll meet <u>here</u> ( ) after the game.

3 Amy works really <u>hard</u> ( ) at school.

4 He felt that he had been <u>unfairly</u> ( ) treated.

5 Paul doesn't feel well <u>today</u> ( ).

6 You can't park <u>there</u> ( ).

Exercise 2.9 Pronouns (section 2.6)

Complete the following sentences by supplying the correct form of the pronoun, as indicated after each sentence. Refer to Table 2.1.

1 The banks gave . . . every opportunity to repay the loan. **Personal, 3rd-person plural.**

2 . . . borrowed more money than necessary. **Personal, 3rd-person singular, masculine.**

3 He only told . . . about it after he got into financial trouble. **Personal, 1st-person plural.**

4 Since the financial meltdown, . . . economy has been struggling. **Possessive, 1st-person plural.**

5 The central bank played . . . part in the recovery. **Possessive, 3rd-person singular, non-personal.**

6 The economy of Iceland was badly hit, but . . . is a special case. **Possessive, 3rd-person plural.**

Exercise 2.10 Pronouns (section 2.6)

Indicate whether the underlined pronouns are personal, possessive, reflexive, demonstrative or relative.

1 <u>It</u> was the worst holiday <u>we</u> ever had.

2 First, <u>our</u> luggage went missing.

3 <u>That</u> was not a good start.

4 Then, <u>our</u> taxi driver took <u>us</u> to the wrong hotel.

5 Then Tom discovered <u>he</u> had lost <u>his</u> passport.

6 So we found <u>ourselves</u> with no luggage, no hotel, and no passport.

7 Eventually, <u>we</u> phoned the travel agent, <u>who</u> was very helpful.

Exercise 2.11 Auxiliary verbs (section 2.7)

Indicate whether the underlined verbs are modal, passive, progressive or perfective auxiliaries.

1 The Internet <u>has</u> revolutionised the way we do business.
2 Now we <u>can</u> order books, theatre tickets and even clothes online.
3 Very soon, every home <u>will</u> have broadband Internet access.
4 The Internet <u>is</u> also changing the way we learn.
5 Online teaching materials <u>can</u> now <u>be</u> accessed from anywhere in the world.
6 In the future, all students <u>may</u> <u>be</u> taught online.
7 However, some teachers believe this <u>would</u> be disastrous for students.
8 They say the Internet <u>should</u> <u>be</u> used sparingly, and that real teachers <u>can</u> never <u>be</u> replaced by computers.
9 For people in remote areas, however, the Internet <u>is</u> really improving their access to education.
10 Distance learning <u>has</u> finally become a reality.

Exercise 2.12 Words and word classes (Chapter 2)

In the space provided, indicate the word class of the underlined words in the following passage. Use the following abbreviations:

Adj = adjective   N = noun
Adv = adverb   Num = numeral
Art = article   P = preposition
Aux = auxiliary verb   Pn = pronoun
C = conjunction   V = verb

Howard Carter is <u>famous</u> ( ) throughout the world as <u>the</u> ( ) man <u>who</u> ( ) discovered the <u>tomb</u> ( ) of the Egyptian king, <u>Tutankamen</u> ( ). <u>His</u> ( ) story <u>is</u> ( ) a <u>very</u> ( ) romantic <u>one</u> ( ), and it <u>has</u> ( ) inspired many Hollywood <u>movies</u> ( ). Carter <u>was</u> ( ) born <u>on</u> ( ) May <u>9th</u> ( ), 1874, in <u>England</u> ( ). His father <u>was</u> ( ) an artist <u>who</u> ( ) specialised in <u>drawing</u> ( ) animal portraits <u>for</u> ( ) <u>local</u> ( ) landowners. <u>He</u> ( ) taught his son the <u>basics</u> ( ) of drawing and painting, <u>and</u> ( ) Howard <u>became</u> ( ) a <u>fairly</u> ( ) accomplished draughtsman. However, his main interest <u>was</u> ( ) in archaeology, and in <u>ancient</u> ( ) Egypt in particular. <u>When</u> ( ) he was just <u>seventeen</u> ( ) years old, Howard sailed <u>to</u> ( ) Alexandria in

Egypt, <u>hoping</u> ( ) to find work as <u>a</u> ( ) draughtsman <u>with</u> ( ) the Egyptian Exploration Fund. His <u>first</u> ( ) job was at Bani Hassan, where he worked <u>under</u> ( ) the famous <u>archaeologist</u> ( ), Flinders Petrie. His role on <u>that</u> ( ) excavation was to <u>copy</u> ( ) the drawings <u>which</u> ( ) <u>were</u> ( ) found <u>on</u> ( ) the walls of the tombs. <u>According to</u> ( ) some sources, Howard worked <u>hard</u> ( ) all day, and then slept in the tombs <u>at</u> ( ) night.

Chapter 3

Phrases

3.1   The five phrase types

When we looked at pronouns (see section **2.6**), we said that they are often used to replace a noun:

David loves football. *He* supports Manchester United.

Here, the personal pronoun *he* replaces the noun *David*. But consider:

The young boy who lives beside us loves football. *He* supports Manchester United.

In this case, *he* replaces the entire sequence *the young boy who lives beside us*. This is not a noun – it is a **noun phrase** (see section **3.2**). We call it a noun phrase because its central word – *boy* – is a noun. More correctly, then, a pronoun can be used to replace a noun phrase.

There are five phrase types:

Phrase type	Examples	Main word
Noun phrase	*the young boy*	noun *boy*
Verb phrase	*has been stolen*	verb *stolen*
Adjective phrase	*very greedy*	adjective *greedy*
Adverb phrase	*too quickly*	adverb *quickly*
Prepositional phrase	*after the storm*	preposition *after*

In a noun phrase, the main word is a noun; in a **verb phrase**, the main word is a verb, and so on. Before looking at each of the five phrase types, a brief note on the word 'phrase'.

In grammar, a 'phrase' can consist of just one word, the main word alone. For instance, we say that both *greedy* and *very greedy* are adjective phrases. Why not simply say that *greedy* is an adjective? This is because the same rules apply to adjectives and adjective phrases. The same positional rules apply to *greedy* and to *very greedy*:

Children can be $\begin{cases} \text{greedy} \\ \text{very greedy} \end{cases}$

Simon was a $\begin{cases} \text{greedy} \\ \text{very greedy} \end{cases}$ child

So, instead of saying each time 'adjective or adjective phrase', it is simpler to say 'adjective phrase' and thereby include adjectives. So, when we talk about phrases, remember that they may consist of just one word.

3.2 Noun phrases

Noun phrases have the following basic structure:

Determiner	Premodifier	Noun	Postmodifier
the	young	*boy*	who lives beside us

3.2.1 Determiners

Determiners introduce noun phrases and come before any Premodifiers that may be present. The most common determiners are the articles (see section **2.10**) – the definite article *the* and the indefinite article *a/an*.

the tree

the books

a newspaper

an optician

Other determiners include:

1 possessive pronouns (see section **2.6.2**):

my books

your ideas

his diet

our house

their problem

2 demonstrative pronouns (see section **2.6.5**):

this book

that car

these buildings

those children

3 numerals (see section **2.11**):

one page

two books

second chance

fourth paragraph

4 *each*, *every*, *all*, *both* and *some*:

each child

every time

all types

some people

both children

5 *many*, *more* and *most*:

many years

more students

most people

With certain restrictions, determiners can co-occur in a noun phrase:

all the children

our first home

every second week

his many talents

all my many relatives

As the examples above show, many determiners express quantity (*all, many, some*) or position in an ordered sequence (*first, next, last*). Determiners are unique to noun phrases. They do not occur in any of the other phrase types. This is because the grammatical role of most determiners is to 'determine' the number (singular or plural) of the noun that follows them. For example:

one + singular:	one *child*
many + plural:	many *children*
every + singular:	every *child*
all + plural:	all *children*

3.2.2 | *Premodifiers*

Premodifiers in a noun phrase occur before the noun and after any determiners that may be present. In a noun phrase, the Premodifier is typically an adjective:

green eyes

a *young* child

some *beautiful* flowers

Premodifiers can co-occur, that is, more than one adjective can premodify the same noun:

lovely green eyes

an *innocent young* child

some *beautiful yellow* flowers

As well as adjectives, the following words can function as Premodifiers in a noun phrase:

1   nouns (see section **2.2**):

bank manager	*bedroom* window
computer manuals	the *Science* Museum

2   genitive nouns (see section **2.2.4**):

David's homework	the *President's* office
the *company's* accounts	our *child's* school

Postmodifiers in a noun phrase occur after the noun and are most commonly prepositional phrases (see section **3.6**) introduced by *of*:

a piece *of cheese*   a box *of chocolates*

a photo *of my dog*   a biography *of Mozart*

a view *of the sea*   the Tower *of London*

The Postmodifier may also be introduced by other prepositions:

the house *on the hill*

the Museum *in Kensington*

the war *between rival street gangs*

a spokesman *for the committee*

the road *to Damascus*

a coat *with a brown collar*

people *without computer skills*

As well as prepositional phrases, Postmodifiers of noun phrases can be:

1   Relative clauses (see section **4.3.2**):

the boy *who lives beside us*

the books *which you bought*

the film *that I enjoyed most*

2   *To*-clauses (see section **4.2**):

a valve *to regulate the airflow*

a place *to store your belongings*

the first man *to walk on the moon*

Postmodifiers in a noun phrase can co-occur. The following examples illustrate noun phrases with two Postmodifiers each:

a holiday [*for two*] [*in Rome*]

the shop [*in the High Street*] [*that sells fish*]

the photograph [*you took*] [*of Napoleon's tomb*]

3.2.4 | *Restrictive and non-restrictive Postmodifiers*

A Postmodifier in a noun phrase may be either restrictive or non-restrictive. A **restrictive** Postmodifer serves to define the noun:

The student *who got the highest grade* was given a prize.

Here, the Postmodifier, *who got the highest grade*, is used to define exactly which student was given a prize. The Postmodifier is therefore strictly necessary to the meaning of the sentence. Compare this with:

The student, *who comes from Birmingham*, was given a prize.

Here, the Postmodifier, *who comes from Birmingham*, does not define exactly which student, from among all the students in the class, was given a prize. It simply conveys additional, optional information. This is a **non-restrictive** Postmodifier.

In writing, non-restrictive Postmodifiers are usually marked off with commas, as in the example above. In speech, the intonation pattern usually indicates their status.

3.2.5 | *Postmodifiers and Complements*

Complements are a type of noun-phrase Postmodifier (see section **3.2.3**), but they have a much closer link with the noun than ordinary Postmodifiers. Compare the following:

1   Postmodifier:

The news *that he gave us today* was welcomed by everyone.

2   Complement:

The news *that he intends to resign* was welcomed by everyone.

In 1, the Postmodifier *that he gave us today* does not define the content of the news. It does not tell us exactly what the news was. In contrast with this, the Complement in 2, *that he intends to resign*, plays a defining role. It tells us precisely what the content of the news was.

The distinction between a Postmodifier and a Complement is not simply one of meaning. There is also a grammatical difference. In the Postmodifier, we can usually replace *that* with *which*:

1a **Postmodifier**:

The news *which he gave us today* was welcomed by everyone.

We cannot replace *that* with *which* in the Complement:

2a **Complement**:

*The news *which he intends to resign* was welcomed by everyone.

In general, nouns that take Complements tend to have abstract reference. Here are some more examples:

the realisation *that it wouldn't work*

the fact *that no one came*

the idea *that countries should cooperate*

the theory *that light is a wave motion*

3.2.6 | *Apposition*

Apposition is a relationship between two noun phrases that have identical reference:

the US President, Barack Obama

The two noun phrases, *the US President* and *Barack Obama*, refer to the same person and are said to be in apposition to each other. Further examples of apposition include:

the Chinese capital, Beijing

John's favourite food, pasta

the head of Microsoft, Bill Gates

our good friends, the Browns

Apposition is often used as a device for clarifying the meaning of the first noun phrase:

the CIA (Central Intelligence Agency)

the larynx (voice box)

230 litres (50 gallons)

In this type of 'clarifying' apposition, the word *or* is sometimes introduced between the two noun phrases:

phototaxis, *or* light-directed motion

vexillology, *or* the study of flags

See also **Pseudo-coordination**, section **4.10**.

Noun phrases are grammatically very versatile. They can perform a wide range of functions in sentence structure (see Chapter 1). We illustrate the main functions of noun phrases here:

1   Subject (see section **1.2**):

> *A large tile* fell from the roof.
>
> *Four people* entered the room.
>
> *The man who lives beside us* is unwell.

2   Subject Complement (see section **1.5**):

> Paul is *my nephew.*
>
> She is *a teacher of English.*
>
> That is *the wrong way to wire a plug.*

3   Direct Object (see section **1.6**):

> The plane left *the runway.*
>
> I bought *a jar of coffee.*
>
> Our teacher writes *detective stories.*

4   Indirect Object (see section **1.7**):

> She told *the chairman* the bad news.
>
> I offered *the girl beside me* a drink.
>
> It gives *people with disabilities* more independence.

5   Object Complement (see section **1.8**):

> He called her *an idiot.*
>
> They appointed him *President of the Board of Trade.*
>
> The trade unions made Britain *the country it is today.*

6   Adjunct (see section **1.12**):

> *Last week,* our freezer broke down.
>
> She's going to Harvard *next year.*
>
> *One day* you'll regret quitting college.

3.3   Verb phrases

A verb phrase consists of a main verb (see section **2.3**), which may be preceded by one or more auxiliary verbs (see section **2.7**):

Auxiliary 1	Auxiliary 2	Auxiliary 3	Main verb
may	have	been	stolen

3.3.1 | The ordering of auxiliary verbs

When two or more auxiliary verbs occur in a verb phrase, they observe the following relative order:

Modal – Perfective – Progressive – Passive

He *may have been being* blackmailed.

However, it is very unusual to find all four of the auxiliary verb types in the same verb phrase, as in this example. More usually, a maximum of two or three auxiliaries will co-occur, as in the following examples:

Modal – Passive:
The seat *can be* lowered.

Progressive – Passive:
This lecture *is being* recorded.

Perfective – Progressive:
She *has been* collecting books for years.

Perfective – Passive:
The deficit *has been* reduced.

Modal – Perfective – Passive:
The concert *should have been* cancelled.

3.3.2 | Tense

Tense refers to the way in which a language expresses the concept of time. In English, there are just two tenses, the present tense and the past tense. In regular verbs, the present tense is expressed by the *-s* form of the verb, when the Subject is third person singular:

3rd-person singular: he *walks*
she *walks*
it/David/the man *walks*

For all other Subjects, the base form of the verb is used:

1st-person singular:	I *walk*
2nd-person singular:	you *walk*
1st-person plural:	we *walk*
2nd-person plural:	you *walk*
3rd-person plural:	they *walk*

On the verb forms, see section **2.3.1**.

The **past tense** is indicated by an *-ed* verb ending, regardless of the Subject:

1st-person singular:	I *walked*
2nd-person singular:	you *walked*
3rd-person singular:	he/she/it/David/the man *walked*
1st-person plural:	we *walked*
2nd-person plural:	you *walked*
3rd-person plural:	they *walked*

In these examples, only a main verb is present, so this verb carries the tense marker. When an auxiliary verb is present, the tense is indicated by the first (or only) auxiliary verb, and not by the main verb:

Present tense:	The chairman *is* speaking.
Past tense:	The chairman *was* speaking.
Present tense:	The ambassador *has* done his duty.
Past tense:	The ambassador *had* done his duty.
Present tense:	A new script *is* being written.
Past tense:	A new script *was* being written.

See also **Finite and non-finite verb phrases**, section **3.3.4**.

3.3.3 | *Expressing future time*

As we saw in section **3.3.2**, English has two tenses, the present tense and the past tense. The *-s* ending indicates present tense, and the *-ed* ending indicates past tense. However, there is no ending to indicate the future, and so it would be incorrect to speak of a 'future tense' in English. In fact, future time is very often expressed by using the present-tense form of a verb:

Peter *arrives* next Friday.

Your flight *leaves* in ten minutes.

David *graduates* in September.

There are several other ways to express **future time** in English:

1   modal auxiliary *will* (see section **2.7.1**):

Peter *will* arrive next Friday.

Your flight *will* leave in ten minutes.

David *will* graduate in September.

The contracted form *'ll* is often used informally:

I*'ll* see you later.

2   semi-auxiliary *be going to* (present tense) (see **2.7.7**):

Peter *is going to* arrive next Friday.

Your flight *is going to* leave in ten minutes.

David *is going to* graduate in September.

3   Progressive auxiliary *be* (present tense) + *-ing* verb (see section **2.7.4**):

Peter *is arriving* next Friday.

Your flight *is leaving* in ten minutes.

David *is graduating* in September.

3.3.4 | *Finite and non-finite verb phrases*

Verb phrases are either finite or non-finite. A verb phrase is **finite** if the first (or only) verb exhibits tense (past or present). The following examples illustrate finite verb phrases. In each case, the finite ('tensed') verb is in italics.

Simon *leaves* work at five.

Simon *left* early yesterday.

Simon *has* left.

Simon *had* left when I arrived.

Simon *has* been leaving early every day.

Notice that when two or more verbs occur in a finite verb phrase (e.g. *has left*, *has been leaving*), only the first verb indicates the tense. All the other verbs have **non-finite** forms. The non-finite verb forms are:

1   the base form, often introduced by *to* (*to leave*);
2   the *-ed* form (*left*);
3   the *-ing* form (*leaving*).

If the first (or only) verb in a verb phrase has one of these forms, then the verb phrase is non-finite:

To *leave* now would be such a pity.

Leaving home can be very traumatic.

Left to himself, Paul copes quite well.

Having left school at 15, David spent years without a job.

In a non-finite verb phrase, all the verbs have a non-finite form. The distinction between finite and non-finite verb phrases is important in the classification of clauses (see section **4.2**).

<hr>

3.3.5 | Aspect

Tense (see section **3.3.2**) refers to the absolute location of an event in time – either past or present. **Aspect** refers to how an event is to be viewed with respect to time. We can illustrate the contrast using the following examples:

1   David *broke* his leg when he was 12.
2   David *has broken* his leg.

In 1, the verb *broke* tells us that David broke his leg in the past (specifically, when he was 12). This is a past-tense verb.

The auxiliary *has*, in 2, is the perfective auxiliary (see **2.7.5**) and it expresses perfective aspect in the verb phrase *has broken*. The verb *has* has present-tense form, and so we can describe the whole verb phrase *has broken* as present tense, perfective aspect.

In 2, the event took place in the past, but it is implied that it took place very recently. It is further implied that it is relevant at the time of speaking (the present) – *David has broken his leg, so call an ambulance (now)!*

The past-tense version of 2 is:

2a David had broken his leg.

Here, the event occurred in the past, but it is implied that it was still relevant at some later time: *David had broken his leg, so he could not play in the Cup Final that year.*

The idea of 'relevance' is important when we wish to distinguish between tense and aspect. Tense alone is exemplified in 1. The event described is wholly in the past, and no current relevance is implied. Both tense and aspect are exemplified in 2 and 2a. In each case, the event described has 'relevance', either in the present, as in 2, or at some time between the event and the present, as in 2a.

The other aspectual auxiliary is the progressive auxiliary *be* (see section 2.7.4):

3   David *is* working in Beijing.
4   David *was* working in Beijing when I met him.

Sentence 3 expresses the idea that the action is still in progress: David is working in Beijing at the time of speaking. For this reason, we say that the sentence exemplifies progressive aspect. Like perfective aspect, progressive aspect also carries an implication of 'relevance'. Here, it is current relevance, at the time of speaking (the present): *David is working in Beijing, so it may be difficult to contact him (now).* The verb phrase *is working* exemplifies present tense, progressive aspect.

Sentence 4 also expresses the idea of action in progress, but at a particular time in the past ('when I met him'). The verb phrase *was working* exemplifies past tense, progressive aspect.

3.3.6 | Mood

Mood refers to distinctions in the form of a verb phrase that express the speaker's attitude towards what is said. There are three moods: indicative, imperative and subjunctive.

1 **Indicative** mood is the most common mood in declarative, interrogative and exclamative sentences (see section **1.15**):

> Paul *enrolled* in a music class.

> *Does* Amy *like* her new school?

> What a big house you *have*!

2 The **imperative** is used in issuing orders:

> *Move* over.

> *Stop* that at once.

3 **Subjunctive** mood is used when we refer to a non-factual or hypothetical situation:

> If I *were* you, I would accept the offer.

> If Sarah Palin *were* President of the USA, what would she do?

This is called the *were*-subjunctive, because the verb phrase consists solely of *were*.

The mandative subjunctive is used after a small number of verbs, including *ask*, *decide*, *insist*, *recommend*, *suggest*, when these verbs are followed by *that*:

> The committee insisted that she *resign* immediately.

> The lawyer asked that he *be* given more time to prepare his case.

The mandative subjunctive is also used after the following adjectives: *crucial*, *essential*, *important*, *necessary*, *vital*:

> It is *important* that every room *be* properly ventilated.

> It is *vital* that prisoners *be* supervised at all times.

The use of the subjunctive is much more common in American English than in British English. In British English, the indicative mood is often preferred:

> If I *was* you, I would accept the offer.

> It is vital that prisoners *are* supervised at all times.

The subjunctive may also be seen in a number of formulaic expressions:

> as it *were*

> *be* that as it may

far *be* it from me

if need *be*

God *be* praised

So *be* it

Come what may

Long *live* the Republic

wish you *were* here

3.4   Adjective phrases

Adjective phrases have the following basic structure:

Premodifier	Adjective	Postmodifier
very	*reluctant*	to leave

The Premodifier in an adjective phrase is most commonly an intensifier (see section **2.5.3**):

fairly new

very useful

extremely cold

In expressions of measurement and age, a noun phrase may function as a Premodifier in an adjective phrase:

three months old

a metre long

10 mm wide

Postmodifiers occur after the adjective:

glad *you could come*

guilty *of murder*

fond *of animals*

happy *to oblige*

delighted *to meet you*

 The functions of adjective phrases

The major functions of adjective phrases are:

1   Subject Complement (see section **1.5**):

> Our aunt is *quite ill*.
>
> You were *very lucky*.
>
> My old teacher seemed *really happy to see me*.

2   Premodifier of a noun (see section **3.2.2**):

> Emily was wearing a *very old* dress.
>
> I've used a *slightly different* recipe this time.
>
> She's a *rather boring* person.

3   Object Complement (see section **1.8**):

> Ice cream always makes Simon *ill*.
>
> The new wallpaper makes the room *much brighter*.
>
> The Gulf Stream keeps our climate *fairly mild*.

3.5   Adverb phrases

Adverb phrases have the following basic structure:

Premodifier	Adverb	Postmodifier
very	*quickly*	indeed

The Premodifier in an adverb phrase is always an intensifier (see section **2.5.3**):

Premodifier	Adverb
very	gradually
too	slowly
extremely	badly
quite	soon

Postmodifiers in adverb phrases are quite rare. Apart from *indeed*, only *enough* is commonly used:

funnily *enough*   oddly *enough*

naturally *enough*   strangely *enough*

3.5.1 | The functions of adverb phrases

The major functions of adverb phrases are:

1   Premodifier of an adjective (see section **2.4**):

David is *extremely* sensitive.

Avatar was a *very* successful film.

The meat was *too* salty.

2   Premodifier of an adverb (see section **2.5**):

I spoke to John *very* recently.

She drives *far too* slowly.

The other witness saw the incident *slightly more* clearly.

3   Adjunct (see section **1.12**):

Suddenly the factory closed and 200 jobs were lost.

Full-time students receive a medical card *automatically*.

He died in his forties *quite recently*.

3.6   Prepositional phrases

Prepositional phrases have the following basic structure:

Premodifier	Preposition	Complement
just	*after*	the game

The Complement in a prepositional phrase is most commonly a noun phrase:

in *London*

around *the world*

across *our street*

through *the open window*

Clauses (see section **4.3**) can also function as the Complement in a prepositional phrase:

It's a good way of *reducing the debt*.

He succeeded by *working hard*.

Prepositional phrases usually consist of a preposition followed by its Complement. Premodifiers in a prepositional phrase are relatively rare, but here are some examples:

just after the game

straight across the road

right around the building

3.6.1 | *The functions of prepositional phrases*

The major functions of prepositional phrases are:

1   Postmodifier of a noun (see section **3.2.3**):

The population *of China* is growing.

The demand *for British steel* has dropped dramatically.

Caroline is reading a book *on Renaissance painting*.

2   Adjunct (see section **1.12**):

I've got to see the doctor *on Wednesday*.

Before the war, he played football for Leeds United.

We met David *beside the river*.

3   Subject Complement (see section **1.5**):

Your lunch is *in the microwave*.

The other gift is *for James*.

Phil Collins was *with a band called Genesis*.

4   Postmodifier of an adjective (see section **3.4**):

   Sarah is very proud *of her achievements.*

   The villagers are not very tolerant *of strangers.*

   The officers were found guilty *of disreputable conduct.*

5   Object Complement (see section **1.8**):

   Sue has a job putting cards *in alphabetical order.*

   I am obliged to place these matters *before the jury.*

   Don't keep me *in suspense.*

Exercises

Exercise 3.1 Noun phrases (section 3.2)

Bracket the noun phrases in each of the following sentences. If a noun phrase has another noun phrase within it, use double bracketing. For example:

   [the old man with [the grey beard]]

1   Strong easterly winds are expected later.
2   The cost of insurance has doubled in the last year.
3   The kids really enjoyed their visit to Disneyland.
4   His first movie was about the siege of Krishnapur.
5   The weapon was found at the bottom of the lake.
6   Harry Potter books are his favourites.
7   The concert was cancelled due to poor ticket sales.
8   The director of the company has resigned.

Exercise 3.2 Determiners (section 3.2.1)

Underline the determiners in the following sentences.

1   His second attempt at the title was much more successful.
2   Many people expected him to win the first race easily.
3   Some people felt that he needed more time to prepare.

4   One journalist even suggested that he should take a break from all competitions.
5   After the second race, he was congratulated by his wife and two children.
6   His many loyal fans chanted his name from the grandstand.
7   The fans will remember that victory for many years.
8   For Roberts, it was an emotional climax to a career that began twenty years earlier.

Exercise 3.3 The ordering of auxiliary verbs (section 3.3.1)

In each of the following sentences, describe the sequence of the underlined auxiliary verbs. For example:

The seat <u>can</u> <u>be</u> adjusted = Modal + Passive

1   All the tickets <u>have</u> <u>been</u> sold.
2   The prize money <u>will</u> <u>be</u> given to charity.
3   The power <u>should</u> <u>be</u> switched off first.
4   You <u>must</u> <u>be</u> joking.
5   The earthquake victims <u>are</u> <u>being</u> rehoused.
6   <u>Have</u> you <u>been</u> talking to Paul?
7   The parents <u>may</u> <u>have</u> <u>been</u> arguing.
8   <u>Could</u> anything else <u>have</u> <u>been</u> done?

Exercise 3.4 Tense (section 3.3.2) and aspect (section 3.3.5)

In each of the following sentences, describe the tense and aspect that are expressed by the underlined auxiliary verb. For example:

The children <u>are</u> leaving = Present tense, Progressive aspect

1   Amy <u>was</u> watching TV when we arrived.
2   Paul <u>is</u> working very hard.
3   The government <u>has</u> supported the banks for years.
4   I <u>have</u> never met your brother.
5   I <u>am</u> looking for a better job.
6   We <u>were</u> staying with friends at the time.
7   The train <u>had</u> already left.
8   All the money <u>has</u> disappeared.

Exercise 3.5 Adjective phrases (section 3.4)

Underline the adjective phrases in the following sentences:

1 In much earlier times Antwerp had been one of the largest cities in western Europe.
2 The vibrant atmosphere of the sprawling city was very exciting for residents and visitors alike.
3 Antwerp became an increasingly important financial centre as time went on.
4 Prices for works of art were incredibly high, and even fairly mediocre artists could make a reasonably good living.
5 The Church was a very significant contributor to the vast wealth of the city.
6 The Bishop of Antwerp commissioned expensive paintings and statues, and the artists were usually very happy to accept the commissions.
7 The Church had always been acutely aware of the need to patronise artists.
8 In turn, the artists produced some of the most magnificent masterpieces that Europe has ever seen.

Exercise 3.6 Adverb phrases (section 3.5)

Underline the adverb phrases in the following sentences:

1 Global warming has recently become a major concern for governments.
2 Previously, many people felt that governments did not take the issue seriously.
3 Now, it seems that the voice of the people is finally being heard.
4 Governments have gradually realised that climate change is a reality.
5 Some governments are obviously uncertain about how to proceed.
6 Many people feel strongly that international cooperation is the only solution.

Exercise 3.7 Prepositional phrases (section 3.6)

Underline the prepositional phrases in the following passage:

Marco Polo was born in Venice in 1254. At that time, Venice was one of Europe's wealthiest cities. At 17, Marco travelled with his father and uncle from Italy to China. That journey eventually opened trade routes between the east and the west. In his book, *The Travels of Marco Polo*, he described the immense size of Chinese cities and the many splendours to be seen at the Emperor's court. His book contains stories about many wonders: bandits in desert hideaways, snakes with legs, and an Emperor who kept a tamed lion at his feet. No one is quite sure how many of these stories are true. Did he really see everything he described, did he hear the stories from other travellers, or did he just make it all up? Some scholars think he never travelled to China at any time. For them, the fact that he never once mentioned tea, the national drink of the Chinese, is proof that his book is a collection of fables. Just before his death, Marco was asked how much of his book was really true. He replied that he had described only half of what he had actually seen.

Chapter 4

Sentences and clauses

This chapter covers three broad areas: **subordination** and **coordination** (see sections **4.1–4.10**); **linking sentences** (see sections **4.11–4.15**); and focusing and **emphasising** (see sections **4.16–4.19**).

4.1 Complex sentences

In Chapter 1, we looked at the simple sentence *Paul plays football*, and we analysed it in terms of the following sentence elements: Subject (S), verb (V) and Direct Object (DO):

S	V	DO
Paul	plays	football.

We also looked briefly at the following sentence:

When the plane landed, the ground crew removed the cargo.

We can analyse this sentence in the same way, in terms of the following sentence elements: Adjunct (A), Subject (S), verb (V) and Direct Object (DO):

A	S	V	DO
When the plane landed	the ground crew	removed	the cargo.

However, unlike the simple sentence, this sentence can be analysed further. This is because the Adjunct (A) *when the plane landed* is itself a 'sentence-like' construction. It has its own Subject, *the plane*, and its own verb, *landed*. Therefore, it displays the sentence pattern S + V. It also has an important additional element: it is introduced by the subordinating conjunction *when* (see section **2.9**).

The presence of the subordinating conjunction indicates that *when the plane landed* is not an independent sentence. It is certainly 'sentence-like', as it displays the sentence pattern S + V, but it cannot stand alone. For this reason, we say that *when the plane landed* is a **subordinate clause**, not a sentence.

A subordinate clause such as *when the plane landed* is a dependent clause – it is part of a larger structure, usually a sentence. In contrast, *the ground crew removed the cargo* can stand alone – it is not subordinate to any higher structure.

A sentence that contains a subordinate clause is called a **complex sentence**.

4.2 Markers of subordination

There are two main indicators that a clause is subordinate:

1   **The presence of a subordinating conjunction**: clauses that are introduced by one of the subordinating conjunctions (see section **2.9**) are subordinate clauses. Here are some examples:

James left the room *because he was angry.*

If you need more money, just phone me.

I read a magazine *while I was waiting.*

However, not all subordinate clauses are introduced by a subordinator. The subordinator *that*, for instance, may be omitted:

Ia Paul knows *that Amy prefers tennis.*

Ib Paul knows *Amy prefers tennis.*

In 1a, *that* indicates that the clause *that Amy prefers tennis* is subordinate. In 1b, however, there is no formal marker of subordination, though the clause *Amy prefers tennis* is still a subordinate clause within the sentence as a whole. Therefore, although a subordinator always indicates a subordinate clause, not all subordinate clauses are introduced by a subordinator.

2   **The form of the verb phrase.** If the verb phrase is non-finite (see section **3.3.4**), then the clause in which it occurs is a subordinate clause. We recall that the non-finite verb forms are (a) the base form (often with *to*), (b) the *-ed* form and (c) the *-ing* form. These three verb forms give their names to three subordinate clause types:

- *to*-clauses:

    The road was widened *to improve the traffic flow.*

    To receive all the channels, you may need an antenna.

    A satellite must reach an altitude of 100 miles *to get clear of the atmosphere.*

- *-ed* clauses:

    Deprived of oxygen, plants will quickly die.

    The warriors faced each other, *dressed in black armour.*

    Designed for drafting, mechanical pencils are also useful for sketching.

- *-ing* clauses:

    Michelangelo painted *lying on his back.*

    The teacher stood in the doorway, *saying nothing.*

    Emily rang the doorbell, *her heart pounding.*

In a *to*-clause, *to* sometimes occurs in the form *in order to* or *so as to*:

In order to reduce heat loss, we've sealed the window frames.

Be punctual *so as to reduce waiting time.*

The form of the verb phrase, then, is a marker of subordination. If the verb phrase is non-finite, the clause that contains it is a subordinate clause.

4.3   Subordinate clause types

The main subordinate clause types are **Adjunct clauses** (see section **4.3.1**), **Relative clauses** (see section **4.3.2**), **Nominal relative clauses** (see section **4.3.3**), *That*-**clauses** (see section **4.3.4**) and **Comparative clauses** (see section **4.3.5**).

4.3.1   *Adjunct clauses*

Adjunct clauses are subordinate clauses that function as Adjuncts in sentence structure (see section **1.12**). They are introduced by a wide range of subordinating conjunctions, including *although, because, if, since, when, while*:

Although he is only 18, he has a very mature attitude.

Sandra left early *because she has an interview tomorrow*.

If you don't hurry you'll miss your flight.

He's lived in the same house *since he was a boy*.

When he was young, Van Gogh loved to paint trees.

I'll watch a DVD *while you're out*.

Adjunct clauses express a very wide range of meanings (see section **4.6**).

4.3.2 | *Relative clauses*

A **relative clause** is introduced by one of the relative pronouns, *that, who, which* or *whose* (see section **2.6.6**):

The book *that I am reading* is fascinating.

The man *who lives beside us* is unwell.

This is a company *which does not exclude people*.

I've got a friend *whose parents are divorced*.

In some circumstances, the relative pronoun may be omitted, leaving a **zero relative clause**:

The book *I am reading* is fascinating.

(cf. The book *that I am reading* . . .)

In another variant, the relative pronoun is again omitted, and the verb has an *-ed* form or an *-ing* form (see section **2.3.1**). This is a **reduced relative clause**:

Houses *built in the 1940s* are usually draughty.

(cf. Houses *which were built in the 1940s* . . .)

The train *arriving at Platform One* is the Cambridge train.

(cf. The train *which is arriving at Platform One* . . .)

4.3.3 | *Nominal relative clauses*

A **nominal relative clause** is introduced by *what, whatever, whoever, where* or *how*:

> *What you need* is a long holiday.

> Take *whatever you want.*

> *Whoever wins the most seats* will form a government.

> This is *where the rebellion started.*

> Laura showed me *how to set the timer.*

As its name suggests, there is a close correspondence between a nominal relative clause and a noun phrase (see section **3.2**):

> *What you need* is a long holiday.

> ~*The thing that you need* is a long holiday.

> Take *whatever you want.*

> ~Take *the thing(s) that you want.*

> *Whoever wins the most seats* will form a government.

> ~*The party that wins the most seats* will form a government.

> This is *where the rebellion started.*

> ~This is *the place where the rebellion started.*

> Laura showed me *how to set the timer.*

> ~Laura showed me *the way to set the timer.*

4.3.4 | **That-*clauses***

A *that*-**clause** is introduced by the subordinating conjunction *that*:

> Everyone knows *that smoking is dangerous.*

> The new ruling means *that pensioners will suffer.*

> Bernard has decided *that he wants to live in Canada.*

It is important to distinguish clearly between the subordinating conjunction *that* and the relative pronoun *that*. Relative pronoun *that* introduces a relative clause, and it can usually be replaced by *which*:

> The book *that I am reading* is fascinating.
>
> ~The book *which I am reading* is fascinating.

In contrast, the subordinating conjunction *that* cannot be replaced by *which*:

> Everyone knows *that smoking is dangerous.*
>
> *~Everyone knows *which smoking is dangerous.*

4.3.5 | *Comparative clauses*

Comparative clauses are introduced by *than* or *as*. Clauses introduced by *than* express comparison in a gradable adjective or adverb:

> Mary is older *than I am.*
>
> It travels faster *than you'd expect.*
>
> Everything is more expensive *than it used to be.*

Comparative clauses introduced by *as* express equivalence:

> Mary is as old *as I am.*
>
> This is as good *as it gets.*
>
> You can be as personal *as you like.*

4.4 Clauses as sentence elements

As elements in sentence structure, subordinate clauses most commonly function as Adjuncts (see section **1.12**). They may also have the following functions:

1 **Subject** (see section **1.2**):

What you need is a long holiday.	nominal relative clause
Leaving home can be very traumatic.	*-ing* clause
To give up now would be such a pity.	*to*-clause
That he should fail to turn up is really annoying.	*that*-clause

With the exception of nominal relatives and *-ing* clauses, clauses functioning as Subjects are relatively rare. The *-ed* type (*Dressed in armour* . . .) cannot function as a Subject. See also **Postponed Subjects**, section **4.18**.

2   **Direct Object** (see section **1.6**):

Paul knows that *Amy prefers tennis.*	*that*-clause
Jim offered *to drive us to the airport.*	*to*-clause
Mary enjoys *visiting art galleries.*	*-ing* clause
We still don't know *what will happen.*	nominal relative clause

3   **Subject Complement** (see section **1.5**):

A detective's first job is *to collect the evidence.*	*to*-clause
The main problem is *finding enough money.*	*-ing* clause
The real reason is *that I can't stand him.*	*that*-clause
That's *what I'm trying to tell you.*	nominal relative clause

4.5   Clauses as phrase elements

When a subordinate clause occurs as an element in a phrase, it most commonly functions as a Postmodifier. Subordinate clauses may occur as Postmodifiers in the following phrase types (the phrases are bracketed):

1   Postmodifier in a noun phrase (see section **3.2.3**):

[The man *who lives beside us*] is unwell.	relative clause
[The man *to ask about plumbing*] is Mr Davis	*to*-clause

That-clauses function as Complements in noun phrases (see section **3.2.5**):

[The fact *that no one came*] is really disappointing.

[The news *that everyone on board was killed*] has just reached us.

2   Postmodifier in an adjective phrase (see section **3.4**):

I wasn't [aware *that I had to register*].	*that*-clause
Chelsea were [reluctant *to admit defeat*].	*to*-clause

3 Complement in a prepositional phrase (see section **3.6**):

> She has a reputation [for *being difficult.*]   *-ing* clause
>
> He's still coming to terms [with *what*   nominal relative clause
> *happened.*]

4.6 The meanings of Adjunct clauses

For the meanings expressed by Adjuncts in a sentence, see section **1.13**. In that section, we identified four major types of Adjunct meaning: time, place, manner and reason. However, when clauses function as Adjuncts, they can express a wider range of meanings. The main types of meaning expressed by Adjunct clauses are shown here:

- Time:

    > I'll speak to you again *before you go.*
    >
    > *When you leave*, please close the door.
    >
    > I'll read the newspaper *while I'm waiting.*

- Condition:

    > I'll be home early *if I can catch the early train.*
    >
    > *Provided he·works hard*, he'll do very well at school.
    >
    > Don't call me *unless it's an emergency.*

- Concession:

    > He paid for the meal, *although he can't really afford it.*
    >
    > *Even though he worked hard*, he failed the final exam.
    >
    > *While I don't agree with her*, I can see why she's angry.

- Reason:

    > Bernard was an hour late *because he missed his train.*
    >
    > I borrowed your laptop, *since you weren't using it.*
    >
    > *As I don't know the way*, I'll take a taxi.

- Result:

    > The kitchen was flooded, *so we had to go to a restaurant.*
    >
    > I've forgotten my password, *so I can't read my email.*
    >
    > Hamilton lost the case, *so he had to pay all the costs.*

- Purpose:

  Leave a window open *to let the steam out.*

  In order to meet growing demand, the BBC introduced a new UHF service.

  You should write down the number *so you won't forget it.*

The type of meaning expressed by an Adjunct clause is often predictable from the subordinating conjunction that introduces it. For instance, *if* always introduces a **conditional clause**, and *because* always introduces a **reason clause**.

However, some subordinating conjunctions can introduce more than one type. *While* can introduce a clause expressing time (*I'll read the newspaper while I'm waiting*) as well as a clause expressing concession (**While I don't agree with her,** *I can see why she's angry*). Similarly, *since* can express time (*He's lived there **since he was a boy***) as well as reason (***Since you can't drive,** you'll have to take a taxi*).

4.7 Peripheral clauses

Peripheral clauses are subordinate clauses that occur within a larger sentence and that are grammatically unintegrated, to varying degrees, in the sentences that contain them.

4.7.1 Comment clauses

A **comment clause** is a brief clause inserted into a sentence, expressing the speaker's attitude towards what is being said:

We could, *I suppose,* share one between us.

So the building was used, *I imagine,* for storing grain.

She was acting on impulse, *I guess.*

I can't help you, *I'm afraid.*

Other comment clauses include: *I assume, I reckon, I should think, I must say, I'm sorry to say, I must admit.*

4.7.2 | Reporting clauses and direct speech

A **reporting clause** identifies the speaker of direct speech:

'The music is too loud', *said Jim.*

The lady said, 'I don't need any help'.

In **direct speech**, the exact words used by a speaker are quoted, as in these examples. In **indirect speech**, the words are subsequently reported by someone else:

Direct speech: 'The music is too loud', said Jim.

Indirect speech: Jim said that the music was too loud.

The switch from direct speech to indirect speech involves a change of tense. Here, the present-tense verb (*is*) in direct speech becomes the past-tense verb (*was*) in indirect speech.

Reporting clauses are often extended by the use of Adjuncts (see section **1.12**):

'The music is too loud', said Jim *angrily.*

'It's a wonderful gift', said Laura *gratefully.*

'I'm not coming back', cried Tom, *as he slammed the door.*

4.7.3 | Tag questions

Particularly in spoken English, questions are often added to the end of a declarative sentence (see section **1.15.1**):

You were born in London, *weren't you?*

The interrogative *weren't you?* is called a **tag question**, because it is 'tagged on' to the end of the declarative *You were born in London*. Tag questions are used to seek agreement with what has just been said in the declarative part. Further examples include:

It's very warm, *isn't it?*

The policy hasn't really worked, *has it?*

Bernard worked in Whitehall, *didn't he?*

If the declarative part is negative, then the corresponding tag question is positive, and vice versa:

It's not too late, *is it?*

It's too late, *isn't it?*

4.7.4 Parentheticals

A **parenthetical** is a complete sentence that is inserted 'parenthetically' into another sentence. In writing, parentheticals are marked off from the main sentence by being enclosed in brackets or dashes:

The range of colours (*most suppliers have 72*) can include metallics and both warm and cool greys.

By Bugatti standards it was not technically advanced – *smaller Bugattis used similar technical layouts* – merely bigger and grander, in all respects.

In speech, parentheticals are sometimes introduced by *and*:

Ronaldo is *and I think most people agree with me* one of the world's greatest footballers.

There is a sense in which *and Hogarth realised this* satire is also a form of entertainment.

4.7.5 Sentential relative clauses

A **sentential relative clause** is introduced by the relative pronoun *which*. Sentential relatives are used to add a comment about what has just been said:

James took an earlier train, *which was lucky for him.*

Mary finally passed her exams, *which was a relief to everyone.*

John doesn't want to meet Laura, *which I can understand.*

4.8 Coordination

Coordination involves using one of the coordinating conjunctions, *and*, *but* and *or* (see section **2.9**), to link items in a sentence. In the following examples, the coordinated items are italicised:

1 *Anthony* and *Caroline* have arrived.
2 She bought *a new dress* and *a handbag*.
3 The house was *old* but *beautiful*.
4 The Centre cares for people who are *mentally* or *physically* disabled.

Items that are linked by a coordinating conjunction are called **conjoins**. In sentences 1 and 2, the conjoins are noun phrases (see section **3.2**), in sentence 3, the conjoins are adjective phrases (see section **3.4**), while, in sentence 4, they are adverb phrases (see section **3.5**).

Coordination can also be used to link clauses:

David drinks wine and *I drink beer.*

The deception was uncovered and *the minister resigned.*

The hotel was lovely but *the weather was awful.*

We can cook at home or *we can go to a restaurant.*

Finally, parts of clauses may be coordinated. The following examples show the coordination of Predicates (see section **1.2**):

James *quit his job* and *moved to Scotland.*

The plane *took off* but *never reached its destination.*

4.9 Coordination types

Coordination normally uses one of the coordinating conjunctions *and*, *but* or *or* to create a link between conjoins:

Quickly *and* resolutely, he strode into the bank.

The course was short *but* intensive.

I don't like laziness *or* dishonesty.

This type of coordination, with a coordinating conjunction actually present, is called **syndetic coordination**.

Coordination can also occur without a coordinating conjunction, as in:

Quickly, resolutely, he strode into the bank.

Coordination without the use of a coordinating conjunction is called **asyndetic coordination.**

When three or more conjoins are coordinated, the coordinating conjunction is usually placed between the final two conjoins only:

We need bread, cheese, eggs, flour *and* milk.

This is syndetic coordination, since a coordinating conjunction, *and*, is present. It would be unusual to find a coordinating conjunction between each pair of conjoins:

We need bread *and* cheese *and* eggs *and* flour *and* milk.

This is called **polysyndetic coordination.** It is usually only used for effect, for instance, to express repetition or continuation:

He just talks *and* talks *and* talks.

I've said it again *and* again *and* again.

This play will run *and* run *and* run.

The coordinators *and* and *or* can be used to link any number of conjoins in coordination. However, *but* is slightly different. It can link a maximum of two conjoins, usually clauses:

Manchester United won the match *but* they lost on aggregate.

4.10   Pseudo-coordination

The coordinators *and* and *or* are sometimes used without any coordinating function:

I'll be there when I'm good *and* ready.

Here, *and* does not coordinate *good* with *ready*. If it did, the sentence would mean something like: *I'll be there when I'm good **and** when I'm ready.* Instead, it means *I'll be there when I'm **completely** ready.* This use of *and* without a coordinating role is called **pseudo-coordination.** Further examples of pseudo-coordination include:

Please try *and* come early.
(= Please try to come early.)

Any more complaints *and* I'm leaving.
(= If I receive any more complaints, I will leave.)

Do that again *and* I'll report you.
(= If you do that again, I will report you.)

When it acts as a coordinator, the conjunction *or* links items that are to be considered as alternatives:

Would you like tea *or* coffee?

You can fly business class *or* economy class.

In the following example, however, the items linked by *or* are not alternatives:

The software is supplied with several useful 'wizards' *or* templates.

Here, *templates* is used to clarify the specialist computer term *wizards*, and so this is a type of apposition (see section **3.2.6**).

4.11 Sentence connectors

Throughout this book, we have taken the sentence as the largest grammatical unit. However, in all forms of continuous communication, both spoken and written, sentences do not operate independently of each other. Instead, effective communication depends to a very large extent on placing sentences in the correct sequence, and on creating meaningful links between them. In this section, we look at some grammatical devices that enable us to create links between sentences in discourse.

There are two main types of sentence connector: logical connectors (see section **4.11.1**) and structural connectors (see section **4.11.2**).

4.11.1 Logical connectors

Logical connectors express a logical relationship between sentences. They express two main types of relationship:

1   **Contrast/concession.** Contrast/concession connectors are used to express a contrast between the information expressed by two sentences:

   The closing date for the receipt of applications is 15 December. *However*, students are advised to submit their applications as soon as possible after 1 September.

It was already clear yesterday that Moscow was losing hope it could persuade the United States and its allies to hold off a ground war for much longer. *Nevertheless*, the Soviet president continued his campaign of high-level diplomacy.

Anybody who says that there is great glory in war is off his head. *On the other hand*, I have to say that war does bring out in people extraordinary nobility.

Other contrast/concession connectors include: *alternatively*, *anyway*, *besides*, *instead*, *nonetheless*, *still*, *yet*.

2   **Result**. Result connectors are used to indicate that the second sentence expresses the result or consequence of what has gone before:

Approval has already been given for a golf course at Smithstown, only three miles away. *Therefore*, an extra facility in the area was considered to be unnecessary.

I have not yet issued you with an invoice for the period prior to Christmas. *Consequently*, I am enclosing an invoice for the total amount of time used so far.

Thousands of commuters have been evacuated from platforms as the police launch a full-scale search. *As a result*, all underground stations with connections to British Rail are also shut.

Other result connectors include: *accordingly*, *hence*, *in consequence*, *so*, *then*, *thus*.

4.11.2 *Structural connectors*

Structural connectors are devices for ordering sentences and paragraphs, and for organising the points we wish to make. Structural connectors are used for the following purposes:

1   **Listing**. Listing connectors are used to list points in a specific order:

First, he cannot stand against the leader unless he is fairly sure of a victory. *Second*, if the Tories lose the next election he will be written out of the succession.

Firstly you have your brakes. *Secondly* you've got the throttle here on the handlebars.

To begin with, turn down the colour control. *Then* manipulate the contrast and brightness controls. *Next*, adjust the opacity of the image.

Other listing connectors include: *in the first place, in the second place, for one thing, for another thing, finally, lastly.*

2 **Adding**. Adding connectors are used to add new information to what has previously been said:

All fatal accidents must be reported immediately to police. *In addition*, the local coroner must be notified.

The Data Protection Act seeks to protect not just data but owners of data. *Furthermore*, it provides guidelines for all users of data.

His remark really shocked me. *Also*, I was baffled by his logic.

Other adding connectors include: *additionally, moreover, what is more, on top of that* (informal), *as well as that.*

3 **Summing up**. 'Summing up' connectors are used to introduce a section that 'sums up' or concludes what has gone before:

In conclusion: the fear of an overwhelming burden of old people is one of the least defensible arguments.

Overall, the policy has been a success.

All in all, he felt he'd had enough.

Other 'summing up' connectors include: *altogether, in sum, in summary, to conclude, to summarise.*

4 **Exemplifying**. Exemplifying connectors introduce examples or instances in support of what has previously been said:

Several new features have been added. *For example*, the display now offers a split-screen view.

Ultraviolet radiation is known to have effects on the immune system. *For instance*, coldsores often occur at the beginning of a summer holiday.

Other exemplifying connectors include: *e.g.* (= *for example*), *i.e.* (= *that is*), *namely.*

4.12   Expressing point of view

Writers can introduce their own point of view very directly by using one of the following:

in my opinion

in my view

as I see it

if you ask me (informal)

In addition, certain adverbs can express the writer's point of view. Usually, an adverb at the start of a sentence describes the action of the verb:

1 *Gradually*, the swelling will disappear.

This can be paraphrased as *The swelling will disappear* **in a gradual manner**.

Compare this with:

2 *Hopefully*, the swelling will disappear.

This cannot be paraphrased as **The swelling will disappear* **in a hopeful manner**. Instead, *hopefully* here expresses the speaker's attitude towards what is being said. So we might paraphrase sentence 2 as: *I hope that the swelling will disappear*.

The italicised adverbs in the following examples also express point of view:

Vincent Van Gogh arrived at the end of the last century to paint his vivid and expressive pictures telling us of his love for the place. *Sadly*, too much sunshine and far too much alcohol got the better of him.

The air mass bringing the coldest temperatures is the polar continental mass. *Fortunately*, it is not that common.

The painting was stolen on Sunday night. *Surprisingly*, no one realised it was missing until Wednesday.

This should have been part of the vision of the new British Steel. *Regrettably*, it wasn't.

Other point-of-view adverbs include: *curiously, frankly, funnily (enough), honestly, ironically, luckily, oddly (enough), predictably, presumably, wisely*.

4.13 Referring expressions

Continuous discourse always contains a great deal of cross-referring from one part of the text to another. In fact, the coherence of a text – whether written or spoken – depends on making unambiguous cross-references between the various parts. To give a simple example:

Simon came home early. *He* was not feeling well.

Here, the personal pronoun *he* refers back to the proper noun *Simon*. The pronoun creates a simple, unambiguous connection between the two sentences. Referring back in this way is called anaphoric reference, or simply **anaphora**. The item that is referred back to is called the **antecedent**. So, in this example, *Simon* is the antecedent of *he*.

Using pronouns is the most common way to make cross-references in a text. The following examples illustrate the use of pronouns to refer back. In each example, the antecedent and its corresponding pronoun are shown in italics.

You should prepare *a study timetable*. You can modify *it* later if you need to.

I like *Johnny Depp*. I saw *him* in Pirates of the Caribbean.

London Underground has announced *the suspension of trains on the Circle Line. This* is due to track maintenance work.

When we feel emotion, *certain involuntary changes* occur within us. *These* include changes in salivation, breathing and heart-rate.

A pronoun can also refer back to the whole of a previous sentence:

Check-in time was ten o'clock. That meant we had to get up at six.

Referring back is the most common type of cross-referencing in a text. However, we can also refer forward:

It's here at last. *The Apple iPad* is finally available in the shops.

Referring forward is called cataphoric reference, or **cataphora**.

4.14   Antecedent agreement

In the sentences

Simon came home early. He was not feeling well.

we say that *Simon* is the antecedent of *he* (see section **4.13**). The pronoun *he* agrees with its antecedent in number (singular), person (third) and gender (masculine). This is called antecedent agreement.

For the purposes of clear communication, it is important to ensure that there is agreement between a pronoun and its antecedent. In the following, there is no agreement:

A good speaker system can be all that's needed to transform your PC from a piece of furniture into an entertainment centre. *They* can give games a lift as much as any posh graphics card.

Since the antecedent *a good speaker system* is singular, we would expect the singular pronoun *it* in the second sentence: *It can give games a lift ...*

Perhaps more importantly for clear communication, the antecedent should be unambiguous:

Laura used to babysit a little girl who kept throwing *her* shoes in the fire.

Here, the antecedent of *her* is ambiguous, since it is unclear exactly whose shoes were thrown in the fire, Laura's or the little girl's. In grammatical terms, is *Laura* or *a little girl* the antecedent of *her*?

4.15   Substitution using *so* and *do*

The word *so* can be used as a substitute for an entire previous sentence:

Q: Will we have time for breakfast at the airport?
A: I hope *so*.
   (= I hope we will have time for breakfast at the airport.)

Using *so* in this way means that we can avoid unwieldy repetition.

The negative counterpart of *so* is *not*:

Q: Is Jim coming tonight?
A: I hope *not*.
   (= I hope Jim is not coming tonight.)

So can also substitute for a phrase:

> The meat was very fresh, and *so* were the vegetables.

Here, *so* substitutes for the adjective phrase *very fresh*. The negative counterpart of phrasal *so* is *neither*:

> The meat was not very fresh, and *neither* were the vegetables.

The verb *do* can also be used as a substitute:

> They asked me to drive them to the airport and I *did*.

Do sometimes combines with *so* as a substitute:

> You should save a little money every month. If you *do so*, you will have no worries.

Here, *do so* substitutes for *save a little money every month*.

4.16 Fronting

Fronting occurs when we move one of the sentence elements from its usual position to the beginning of the sentence. Consider the following simple sentence:

> David (S) owes (V) £4,000 (DO).

The Direct Object *£4,000* can be 'fronted' as follows:

> £4,000 (DO) David (S) owes (V).

Fronting gives special emphasis to the fronted element. In this example, it might be used to express astonishment at the amount of money that David owes. The following examples also contain fronted Direct Objects:

> *Ice-cream* he wants! (cf. He wants *ice-cream*.)

> *Some games* we won easily. (cf. We won *some games* easily.)

> *That much* I understand. (cf. I understand *that much*.)

A Subject Complement (see section **1.5**) may also be fronted:

> *Stone cold* her hands were. (cf. Her hands were *stone cold*.)

> *Extremely rude* she was. (cf. She was *extremely rude*.)

4.17 Cleft sentences

The simple sentence *Simon studied French last year* can be rewritten as:

It was Simon who studied French last year.

This is called a **cleft sentence**, because the original simple sentence has been divided (or 'cleft') into two clauses:

Clause 1: It was Simon

Clause 2: who studied French last year

A cleft sentence is used when we wish to emphasise one element of the original sentence, often as a way of excluding other possibilities:

It was *Simon* who studied French last year (not *Amy*).

Here, *Simon*, the Subject of the original sentence, is emphasised. We can also emphasise other elements, including the Direct Object *French*:

It was *French* that Simon studied last year (not *German*).

Finally, we can emphasise the Adjunct *last year*:

It was *last year* that Simon studied French (not *this year*).

The emphasised element in a cleft sentence is called the **focus**. Cleft sentences are introduced by *it*, and the verb is always *be*. Therefore, the pattern of a cleft sentence is:

It	Be	Focus	Clause
It	was	Simon	who studied French last year.

4.18 Postponed Subjects

The Subject is usually the first element in a sentence. However, if the Subject is a clause, it may be postponed to the end:

It's not surprising that James failed his exams.

Here, the Subject is the *that*-clause *that James failed his exams*. The Subject has been postponed to the end of the sentence, and its normal position is filled by *it*. This use of *it* is called **anticipatory it**, because it 'anticipates' the postponed Subject. In the more typical pattern, with the Subject at the beginning, this sentence sounds stylistically awkward:

That James failed his exams is not surprising.

To-clauses may be postponed in the same way:

> It was a good idea *to bring an umbrella*.

> (cf. *To bring an umbrella* was a good idea.)

It is particularly desirable, from a stylistic viewpoint, to postpone a Subject clause when it is very long:

> It soon came to our attention that no one from the area had actually applied for any type of housing benefit.

> (cf. That no one from the area had actually applied for any type of housing benefit soon came to our attention.)

Postponing the Subject is not always just a matter of style. With some verbs, postponement is obligatory:

> It seems that many people are deeply attached to the monarchy.

> *~That many people are deeply attached to the monarchy seems.

> It appears that his statement had wider implications.

> *~That his statement had wider implications appears.

> It turned out that his secretary had stolen the money.

> *~That his secretary had stolen the money turned out.

4.19   *There*-sentences

There-sentences are introduced by the word *there*:

> There is a man at the door.

> There is a God after all.

> There was a phonecall for you.

> There is no such thing as a popular tax.

There-sentences are chiefly used to introduce new information relating to the existence – or non-existence – of some state of affairs. For this reason, they are sometimes called 'existential' sentences.

The word *there* in these constructions should be clearly distinguished from the adverb *there*, which denotes place and which can be contrasted with the adverb *here*:

> There he is. (cf. He is *there*.)

> Here he is. (cf. He is here.)

Exercises

Exercise 4.1 Complex sentences (section 4.1)

In each of the following sentences, underline the subordinate clauses:

1 An earthquake has struck the mountainous region of Qinghai, China, killing over 600 people.
2 Local authorities estimate that around 9,000 people have been injured.
3 Rescue attempts are difficult because the area is very remote.
4 The disaster struck on Wednesday, when the quake shook the entire region.
5 Many houses have collapsed in the township of Jiegu, leaving their occupants homeless.
6 In order to reach some victims, rescuers must tunnel through several metres of debris.
7 The central government in Beijing has praised the rescuers, who are working throughout the night.
8 While aftershocks continue, more and more bodies are being found.

Exercise 4.2 Subordinate clause types (section 4.3)

Indicate whether the underlined clauses are Adjunct clauses, relative clauses, or nominal relative clauses.

1 The man standing next to the President is his Chief of Staff.
2 He is the man who is responsible for all White House staff.
3 What every President needs most is someone to organise his timetable.
4 President Reagan knew all his staff by their first names, as though he had hired them himself.
5 If the President leaves the White House, he is usually accompanied by the press.
6 President Obama caused panic among security when he slipped out to his daughter's football game.
7 It takes most Presidents some time to learn how to handle all their responsibilities.

Exercise 4.3 Clauses as sentence elements (section 4.4)

Indicate the function of the underlined clauses in the following sentences:

1 That is <u>how most people first get involved with drugs</u>.
2 Nobody wants <u>to become a drug addict</u>.
3 Most young people don't even realise <u>that drugs can kill you</u>.
4 For some people, <u>saying 'no'</u> is not as easy as it sounds.
5 <u>To avoid conflict at home</u>, some parents just ignore the problem.
6 <u>To criticise all parents on these grounds</u> is a bit harsh.
7 Teenagers simply don't like <u>being criticised</u>.
8 Uncritical advice is <u>what they need</u>.

Exercise 4.4 Clauses as phrase elements (section 4.5)

Indicate the function of each of the following underlined clauses:

1 The patient is unable <u>to move his legs</u>.
2 My brother has invented a new way of <u>developing photographs</u>.
3 Some children are afraid <u>to go to sleep at night</u>.
4 Following several unsuccessful attempts <u>to restore peace</u>, a ceasefire was finally signed.
5 A man <u>who tried to steal a police car</u> has been detained for questioning.
6 The UN considered a suggestion <u>that German soldiers should be part of the peace-keeping troop</u>.
7 All investors are anxious <u>to get their money back</u>.

Exercise 4.5 The meanings of Adjunct clauses (section 4.6)

Indicate the kind of meaning expressed by the underlined Adjunct clauses.

1 <u>When the Christmas lights were switched on</u>, everyone gasped in amazement.
2 <u>Though I couldn't see her face</u>, I knew it was Amy.
3 Paul has played music <u>since he was six years old</u>.
4 <u>If anyone phones</u>, say I'm not here.
5 I'll make you a veggie burger, <u>since you don't eat meat</u>.
6 I read an old copy of Newsweek <u>while I was waiting</u>.
7 The microphone wasn't working <u>so no one could hear him</u>.

Exercise 4.6 Coordination (section 4.8)

Underline the conjoins in each of the following sentences:

1 The forensics team examined the evidence carefully and methodically.
2 You will have to wait two or three weeks for a visa.
3 He works during the day and goes to classes at night.
4 You have to consider your own interests and other people's interests.
5 Voting ends at 9 p.m., but the result won't be known for 48 hours.
6 The dog ran out the door and across the road.
7 My car is very old but in good condition.

Exercise 4.7 Referring expressions (section 4.13) and Antecedent agreement (section 4.14)

In each of the following, underline the antecedent of the italicised referring expressions:

1 The prize was awarded jointly to Paul and Amy. *They* got exactly equal marks in the exam.
2 Everyone thinks that winning the Lottery would be marvellous, but *it* can also cause a lot of problems.
3 The drug may have some unexpected side effects. *These* may include inflammation and nausea.
4 Countries throughout western Europe closed their airspace. *That* had never happened before.
5 The climbers left most of *their* equipment at a base camp before setting out.
6 The customer slowly buttered his toast before spreading *it* lavishly with marmalade.
7 The Metropolitan Police and the Serious Fraud Office have uncovered between *them* financial malpractice in the gaming industry.

Exercise 4.8 Substitution using so and do (section 4.15)

In each of the following, underline the expression that is being substituted by the italicised *so* or *do so*:

1 Paul is a teacher, and *so* is his wife.
2 Charles was delighted with the gift, and *so* was Amy.

3 Doctors used to drain a patient's blood using leeches, but they don't *do so* any longer.
4 He wanted me to lie about my tax returns, but I was not prepared to *do so*.
5 You can transfer part of the money to a trust fund, if you *so* wish.
6 I was not very happy with the service, and I told them *so*.
7 Macbeth has an extraordinary capacity to delude himself. *So* too has Othello.

Exercise 4.9 Postponed Subjects (section 4.18)

Rewrite each of the following sentences so that they have a postponed Subject and begin with anticipatory *it*:

1 To worry about the future is perfectly normal.
2 That the children should have adequate food and clothing is very important.
3 Whether or not they qualify for subsidised housing is unclear at this stage.
4 That climate change is a reality is now undisputed.
5 To use an electric blender is so much more convenient.

Chapter 5

Word formation and spelling

5.1 The structure of words

Many words in English have a recognisable internal structure. For example, the word *unsuccessful* can be broken down into the following three parts:

un + success + ful

The first part, *un-*, is called the **prefix**. The second part, *success*, is a complete word in itself, and is called the **base**. The last part, *-ful*, is called the **suffix**.

Prefix	**Base**	**Suffix**
Un	success	ful

Prefixes and suffixes are added to existing words to create new words.

5.2 Prefixes

Prefixes are added to the beginning of a word to create a new word. They contribute specific types of meaning. For instance, when we add the prefix *pre-* to the word *1945*, we create a new word *pre-1945*, meaning *before 1945*. The following are the main prefixes used in English, together with the kinds of meaning they contribute.

anti-	against, opposed to	*anti-depressant, anti-nuclear, anti-war, anti-Western*
de-	to reverse something	*decriminalise, de-activate, de-commission, deform*
dis-	reverse of	*disagreement, disapprove, dislike, disqualify*
	remove something	*disambiguate, disarm, disenfranchise, dislodge*

extra-	beyond	extraterrestrial, extra-curricular, extra-mural, extra-sensory
il-, im-	not	illegal, illegible, illegitimate, impatient, impossible, impolite
in-, ir-		inappropriate, inconceivable, intolerant, irregular, irrelevant, irresponsible
inter-	between	international, inter-racial, intergalactic, interwoven
mis-	to do something badly or incorrectly	miscalculate, misconstrue, miskick, misunderstand
non-	not	non-European, non-resident, non-stick, non-white
post-	after	post-1945, postgraduate, post-colonial, post-war
pre-	before	pre-1914, pre-war, predetermined, pre-set
pro-	in favour of	pro-life, pro-democracy, pro-Europe
re-	to do something again	re-apply, re-design, re-introduce, repaint
un-	reverse of	unclear, undemocratic, unnecessary, unusual,
	remove something	undress, unleash, unmask, unscrew

5.3 Suffixes

Suffixes are added to the end of a word to create a new word. Certain suffixes are associated with certain word classes. For instance, the suffix -able appears at the end of many adjectives, including reasonable, remarkable, believable. The suffix -ist is used to create many nouns, including capitalist, physicist, specialist. The following are the most common suffixes associated with the major word classes.

1 Noun suffixes:

-age	blockage, drainage, postage, spillage
-al	betrayal, dismissal, recital, removal

-ant	*claimant, contestant, inhabitant, informant*
-dom	*freedom, kingdom, martyrdom, officialdom*
-ee	*absentee, employee, refugee, trainee*
-er/-or	*actor, blender, defender, eraser, teacher*
-ism	*ageism, favouritism, racism, terrorism*
-ist	*artist, cyclist, motorist, perfectionist*
-ity	*opportunity, publicity, responsibility, severity*
-ment	*embarrassment, environment, equipment, government*
-ness	*coolness, dryness, smoothness, willingness*
-ship	*citizenship, dictatorship, hardship, relationship*
-tion	*demonstration, ignition, migration, recreation*

2 Adjective suffixes:

-able	*achievable, profitable, reasonable, remarkable*
-al	*accidental, industrial, musical, physical, whimsical*
-ful	*grateful, hopeful, successful, tuneful, useful*
-ish	*amateurish, childish, feverish, foolish, ghoulish*
-less	*careless, homeless, hopeless, painless, restless*
-like	*apelike, childlike, godlike, starlike*
-y	*cloudy, creepy, funny, rainy, sleepy*

3 Verb suffixes:

-ate	*adjudicate, congratulate, hyphenate, populate*
-en	*broaden, deafen, ripen, sadden, tighten, widen*
-ify	*amplify, beautify, clarify, classify, identify, purify*
-ise/-ize	*economise, modernise, popularise, realise, terrorize*

4 Adverb suffixes:

-ly	*brilliantly, carefully, slowly, smoothly, terribly*
-wards	*afterwards, backwards, onwards, upwards*
-wise	*anticlockwise, clockwise, health-wise, relationship-wise*

5.4 Compounding and blending

Compounding involves combining two bases (see section **5.1**) to create a new word. For instance, the bases *head* and *ache* combine to form *headache*. Further examples of compounding include:

chair + person	=	*chairperson*
green + house	=	*greenhouse*
help + line	=	*helpline*
key + board	=	*keyboard*
life + style	=	*lifestyle*
match + box	=	*matchbox*
news + paper	=	*newspaper*
post + card	=	*postcard*

Many adjectives are formed by compounding a noun with the *-ed* or *-ing* form of a verb (see section **2.3.1**), as set out below.

Noun		-ed/-ing verb		Adjective
drug	+	induced	=	*drug-induced*
poverty	+	stricken	=	*poverty-stricken*
battery	+	operated	=	*battery-operated*
stress	+	related	=	*stress-related*
rat	+	infested	=	*rat-infested*
award	+	winning	=	*award-winning*
eye	+	catching	=	*eye-catching*
fun	+	loving	=	*fun-loving*
penny	+	pinching	=	*penny-pinching*
time	+	consuming	=	*time-consuming*

See also **Participial adjectives** (section **2.4.3**).

Blending is similar to compounding, except that only parts of existing words are combined to create a new word. For example, the word *camcorder* is formed by combining *cam* (from *camera*) with *corder* (from *recorder*). Other examples of blending include:

bionic	=	*biological* + electro*nic*
biopic	=	*biographical* + *pic*ture
cyborg	=	*cyb*ernetic + *org*anism
docudrama	=	*docu*mentary + *drama*
docusoap	=	*docu*mentary + *soap* opera
ecoterrorism	=	*eco*logy + *terrorism*
edutainment	=	*edu*cation + enter*tainment*
e-zine	=	*e*lectronic + maga*zine*
heliport	=	*heli*copter + air*port*
infotainment	=	*info*rmation + enter*tainment*
motel	=	*mot*or + ho*tel*
netiquette	=	Inter*net* + *etiquette*
netizen	=	Inter*net* + ci*tizen*
paratroopers	=	*para*chute + *troopers*
pulsar	=	*puls*ating + st*ar*
sci-fi	=	*sci*ence + *fi*ction
simulcast	=	*simul*taneous + broad*cast*
smog	=	*sm*oke + f*og*

5.5   Acronyms, abbreviations and clipping

Acronyms are formed by combining the initial letters or syllables of two or more words. The combination is pronounced as a single word:

AIDS	*a*cquired *i*mmune *d*eficiency *s*yndrome
BIOS	*B*asic *I*nput *O*utput *S*ystem
DOS	*D*isk *O*perating *S*ystem
FAQ	*f*requently *a*sked *q*uestions
laser	*l*ight *a*mplification by *s*timulated *e*mission of *r*adiation
Oxfam	*Ox*ford Committee for *Fam*ine Relief

radar	*radio detecting and ranging*
RAM	*random access memory*
ROM	*read-only memory*
SAD	*seasonal affective disorder*
SALT	*Strategic Arms Limitation Treaty*
SatNav	*satellite navigation system*
scuba	*self-contained underwater breathing apparatus*
UNPROFOR	*United Nations Protection Force*
WYSIWYG	*What You See Is What You Get*

Abbreviations are also formed from the initial letters of words, but, unlike acronyms, they are spoken by spelling out each letter:

ATM	*automated teller machine*
BST	*British Standard Time*
cpu	*central processing unit*
DNA	*deoxyribonucleic acid*
GPS	*global positioning system*
HIV	*human immunodeficiency virus*
HTML	*hypertext markup language*
http	*hypertext transfer protocol*
ISD	*international subscriber dialling*
IT	*information technology*
o.g.	*own goal*
OTT	*over the top*
PC	*personal computer (also political correctness)*
PRP	*performance-related pay (also profit-related pay)*
RSI	*repetitive strain injury*
UFO	*unidentified flying object*
UNHCR	*United Nations High Commission for Refugees*

URL	*Universal Resource Locator*
WWF	*World Wildlife Fund*
WWW	*World Wide Web*

The following abbreviations are now widely used in e-mail messages and in online discussion groups:

AFK	*away from keyboard*
BTW	*by the way*
FWIW	*for what it's worth*
FYI	*for your information*
IMHO	*in my humble opinion*
IMO	*in my opinion*
LOL	*laughing out loud*

Clipping is a type of abbreviation in which one or more syllables are omitted or 'clipped' from a word. Most commonly, the beginning of the word is retained:

ad (also *advert*)	advertisement
decaff (also *decaf*)	decaffeinated coffee
demo	demonstration
exam	examination
fax	facsimile
gym	gymnastics (also gymnasium)
lab	laboratory
memo	memorandum
movie	moving picture
photo	photograph
pop	popular music

Clipping is a very common method of creating familiar personal names, including *Fred* (from *Frederick*), *Tim* (from *Timothy*) and *Seb* (from *Sebastian*).

Back formations

Back formations are words (usually verbs) formed by removing from a noun what is thought to be a suffix, and adding a verb ending. In the following, the right-hand column shows the word from which the back formation is derived.

emote	*emotion*
enthuse	*enthusiasm*
liaise	*liaison*
prioritise	*priority*
sculpt	*sculptor*
televise	*television*

The verb *legitimise* is formed by back formation from the adjective *legitimate*.

Combining forms

Combining forms are segments that do not exist as words in their own right, but carry a specific meaning when they are combined with other segments. They are added to the beginning or end of another segment or word to create a new word. The following combining forms have been especially productive in recent years:

bio-	*biodiversity, bioethics, biohazard, biosphere*
cyber-	*cybernaut, cybernetics, cyberspace*
e-	*e-mail/email, e-business, e-commerce, e-text*
Euro-	*Eurocrat, Eurosceptic, Eurostar, Eurotunnel*
hyper-	*hyperlink, hypermarket, hypermedia, hypertext*
mega-	*megabucks, megabyte, megastar, megastore*
techno-	*technobabble, technocrat, technojunkie, techno-pop*
tele-	*telecottage, telematics, teleworking, telemarketing*
-ware	*freeware, groupware, hardware, shareware, software*

5.8 Inflections

Inflections are a special type of suffix (see section **5.3**). They are added to the end of a word to indicate a grammatical property. For instance, the -*s* inflection is added to a noun to indicate plural number (*tree/trees*).

Inflections differ from other suffixes in one important respect. The suffix -*ment*, for example, added to the verb *embarrass* creates a completely different word, the noun *embarrassment*. Adding an inflection, however, does not create a new word, but a different grammatical form of the same word. For example, the words *tree* and *trees* are two forms of the same lexical word *tree*. In a dictionary, they would both appear under *tree*. They differ only in number: *tree* is singular, and *trees* is plural.

In comparison with other languages, English has relatively few inflections. They are always suffixes; that is, they are always added to the end of a word. The inflections are shown in Table 5.1.

Table 5.1 Inflections

	Inflection		Examples
Nouns	plural number	-*s*	trees
	genitive	-'*s*	John's car
		-'	the boys' school
Main verbs	-*s* form (3rd-person singular)	-*s*	walks
	past form	-*ed*	walked
	-*ed* form	-*ed*	walked
	-*ing* form	-*ing*	walking
Adjectives and adverbs	comparative	-*er*	older, sooner
	superlative	-*est*	oldest, soonest

5.9 Adding inflections: general spelling rules

There are four general spelling rules for adding inflections. These are set out below:

1 **Spelling rule 1.** Double the final consonant before adding *-ed*, *-ing*, *-er* or *-est*:

Verb	+ -ed	+ -ing
rub	rubbed	rubbing
stop	stopped	stopping
gag	gagged	gagging
jam	jammed	jamming
plan	planned	planning
occur	occurred	occurring
regret	regretted	regretting

Adjective	+ -er	+ -est
red	redder	reddest
big	bigger	biggest
grim	grimmer	grimmest
wet	wetter	wettest

- In British English, verbs ending in *-el* double the *l*:

travel	travelled	travelling
marvel	marvelled	marvelling

However, in American English, the final *l* is not doubled:

travel	traveled	traveling
marvel	marveled	marveling

- Final *l* is not doubled when it follows *a* or *o*:

conceal	concealed	concealing
reveal	revealed	revealing
cool	cooled	cooling

- Final *g* is not doubled when it follows *n*:

strong	stronger	strongest
young	younger	youngest

2 **Spelling rule 2.** Change final *y* to *i* before adding *-s*, *-ed*, *-er* or *-est*:

Verb	**+ -s**	**+ -ed**
cry	cries	cried
occupy	occupies	occupied
try	tries	tried
worry	worries	worried

Adjective	**+ -er**	**+ -est**
easy	easier	easiest
funny	funnier	funniest
heavy	heavier	heaviest
weary	wearier	weariest

Adverb	**+ -er**	**+ -est**
early	earlier	earliest

If the final *y* follows a vowel, then it is retained:

convey	conveys	conveyed
delay	delays	delayed
play	plays	played
enjoy	enjoys	enjoyed

The verbs *lay*, *pay* and *say* do not take an *-ed* ending:

lay	lays	laid
pay	pays	paid
say	says	said

3 **Spelling rule 3.** Drop silent *e* before adding *-ed*, *-ing*, *-er* or *-est*:

Verb	**+ -ed**	**+ -ing**
care	cared	caring
change	changed	changing
hope	hoped	hoping
love	loved	loving

Adjective	**+ -er**	**+ -est**
blue	bluer	bluest
close	closer	closest
large	larger	largest
whitest	whiter	whitest

- If the base ends in *ie*, change *ie* to *y* before adding *-ing*:

die	dying
lie	lying
tie	tying

- The *e* is retained in *dyeing* and *canoeing*.

4 **Spelling rule 4.** Add *e* before *-s* if the base ends in one of the following: *s*, *sh*, *ch*, *tch*, *x* or *z*:

Verb	**+ s**
pass	passes
push	pushes
teach	teaches
catch	catches
relax	relaxes
buzz	buzzes

Noun	**+ s**
mass	masses
box	boxes
church	churches
match	matches
wish	wishes
quiz	quizzes

On irregular noun plurals, see section **5.11**.

5.10 Adding *-ly* and *-ally*

Many adverbs are formed by adding *-ly* to an adjective:

Adjective	**Adverb**
quiet	quietly
recent	recently
soft	softly

If the adjective already ends in *y*, change *y* to *i*:

Adjective	Adverb
steady	steadily
weary	wearily

However, if the adjective ends in *-ic*, add *-ally* (not *-ly*) to form the adverb:

Adjective	Adverb
basic	basically
dramatic	dramatically
enthusiastic	enthusiastically
emphatic	emphatically
genetic	genetically
linguistic	linguistically
realistic	realistically
scientific	scientifically
specific	specifically

The adverb *publicly* (from the adjective *public*) is an exception to this rule.

5.11   Plural nouns

Regular nouns form the plural by adding *-s* to the singular form:

Singular	+ *s*	= Plural
table	+ *s*	= tables
truck	+ *s*	= trucks
elephant	+ *s*	= elephants

Some plurals are formed by changing the singular ending in an irregular way:

-y → -ies	ability → *abilities*
	memory → *memories*
	party → *parties*

-s → -es	cross → *crosses*
	loss → *losses*
	mass → *masses*
-f or -fe → -ves	thief → *thieves*
	shelf → *shelves*
	life → *lives* (but note: *lowlife* → *lowlifes*)
-on → -a	criterion → *criteria*
	phenomenon → *phenomena*
-um → -a	bacterium → *bacteria*
	millennium → *millennia*
-us → -i	focus → *foci*
	nucleus → *nuclei*
-a → -ae	amoeba → *amoebae*
	formula → *formulae*
-is → -es	analysis → *analyses*
	crisis → *crises*
-ex or -ix → -ices	index → *indices*
	matrix → *matrices*

Nouns ending in -*o* generally take the -*os* endng in the plural form (*photos, radios, videos*), but, in some older words, the plural is formed by changing -*o* to -*oes*:

-o → -oes	echo → *echoes*
	hero → *heroes*
	tomato → *tomatoes*

5.12   Variants with *s* or *z*

Many words can be spelled with either -*s*- or -*z*-:

-s- *variant*	**-z- *variant***
criticise	criticize
finalise	finalize
organise	organize
organisation	organization

polarise	polarize
realise	realize
realisation	realization

Both variants are acceptable, though, in general, American English prefers the -z- variant, while British English prefers the -s- variant.

No choice is available in the following words, which are always spelled with -s-:

advise	exercise
arise	guise
chastise	revise
comprise	rise
despise	supervise
disguise	surprise
enterprise	wise

5.13   British and American spelling variants

Spelling differences between British English and American English are not as widespread as is often thought. The vast majority of words have the same spelling in both varieties. However, the following systematic spelling differences may be observed:

	British English	American English
-our/-or	behaviour	behavior
	colour	color
	favourite	favorite
	humour	humor
	labour	labor
	neighbour	neighbor
-re/-er	centre	center
	fibre	fiber
	theatre	theater
	litre	liter
	metre	meter

-ogue/-og	analogue	analog
	catalogue	catalog
	dialogue	dialog
-ae, -oe/-e	anaemia	anemia
	anaesthesia	anesthesia
	diarrhoea	diarrhea
	foetus	fetus
	haemorrhage	hemorrhage
-ence/-ense	defence	defense
	offence	offense
	pretence	pretense
miscellaneous	aluminium	aluminum
	cheque	check
	jewellery	jewelry
	kerb	curb
	manoeuvre	maneuver
	mould	mold
	plough	plow
	tyre	tire
	sulphur	sulfur

5.14 Problem spellings

Even the most experienced writers have difficulties with the spelling of some words. This is especially true in the case of pairs, such as *it's* and *its*, which sound alike but have different spellings and meanings. In this section, we disambiguate the most troublesome of these pairs.

accept/except:

Accept is a verb: *You should accept his offer.*

Except is a preposition (see section 2.8): *I like all types of music except jazz.*

advice/advise:

Advice is a noun: *Ask your teacher for advice.*

Advise is a verb:

His doctor *advised* him to stop smoking.

affect/effect:

Affect is a verb: *Pollution in the atmosphere **affects** our climate.*

Effect is a noun: *What **effect** does pollution have?* Effect is sometimes used as a verb, meaning to bring about (change): *The National Health Service has **effected** huge social change in Britain.*

altar/alter:

Altar is a noun: *The sacrifice was placed on the **altar**.*

Alter is a verb, meaning to change: *It's too late now to **alter** your holiday plans.*

choose/chose:

Both are forms of the same verb, *choose*, meaning 'to select'.

Choose is the base form (see section **2.3.2**): ***Choose** your clothes carefully. It is difficult to **choose**.*

Chose is the past form (see section **2.3.4**): *We **chose** a site overlooking the valley.* The -ed form of this verb is *chosen*: *Rio Ferdinand was **chosen** as the new captain of England.*

council/counsel/councillor/counsellor:

Council is a noun, meaning 'board or managing committee': *The local **council** has introduced parking restrictions.* A member of a council is a *councillor*.

Counsel is a verb, meaning 'to guide or advise', usually in relation to behaviour: *They hired a social worker to **counsel** the children.* The corresponding nouns are *counsellor*, meaning 'someone who gives advice', and *counsel*, meaning 'advice or guidance': *The teacher gave us good **counsel**.*

discreet/discrete:

Both are adjectives. Discreet means 'tactful': *I've made some **discreet** enquiries.* The corresponding noun is *discretion*.

Discrete means 'separate, distinct': *The country is divided into two **discrete** political regions.* The corresponding noun is *discreteness*.

its/it's:

Its is a possessive pronoun (see section **2.6.2**): *The horse shook **its** head.*

It's is a contraction of *it is*: ***It's** a lovely day*, or *it has*: ***It's** been ages since we met.*

licence/license:

In British English, *licence* is a noun, as in *driving licence*, and *license* is a verb, meaning *to give permission*: *The restaurant is **licensed** to sell spirits.*

Licence does not exist in American English; *license* is used as the noun and as the verb.

loose/lose:

Loose is an adjective, meaning 'not tight': *The seatbelt is too **loose**.* The corresponding verb is *loosen*: *You can **loosen** your seatbelts now.*

Lose is a verb, meaning 'to mislay': *Be careful not to **lose** your passport*, or 'not win': *If United **lose** this game their season is over.*

personal/personnel:

Personal is an adjective: *You shouldn't ask **personal** questions.*

Personnel is a noun, meaning 'staff': *All **personnel** should report to reception.*

practice/practise:

Practice is a noun, meaning (a) 'training for sport, music etc.': *I've got football **practice** at six o'clock*; (b) 'the exercise of a profession', e.g. *medical **practice**, legal **practice**.*

In British English, *practise* is a verb: *Amy **practised** her speech in front of a mirror.*

The word *practise* does not exist in American English; *practice* is used as the noun and as the verb.

principal/principle:

Principal is most commonly used as an adjective, meaning 'most important': *The government's **principal** concern should be unemployment.* As a noun, *principal* refers to the most important, or highest-ranked, person in an organisation, e.g. ***Principal** of a school.*

Principle is a noun, meaning *rule of conduct: a person of **principle**, moral **principles**.*

quiet/quite:

Quiet is an adjective meaning *silent: a **quiet** child, keep **quiet**.*

Quite is an intensifier (see section **2.5.3**) and is used before an adjective or an adverb: *It's **quite** cold outside, I spoke to James **quite** recently.*

stationary/stationery:

> *Stationary* is an adjective meaning 'not moving': *a **stationary** vehicle.*

> *Stationery* is a noun, referring to pens, paper, stickynotes etc.

than/then:

> *Than* is used in comparative constructions (see section **4.3.5**): *Paul is older **than** Amy, The professor is younger **than** I expected.*

> *Then* is an adverb of time: *We toured the museum and **then** we went home.* As a sentence connector (see section **4.11**), *then* means 'in that case': *Do you like horror films? **Then** you'll love Poltergeist.*

their/there/they're:

> *Their* is a possessive pronoun (see section **2.6.2**): *The children love **their** toys.*

> *There* is an adverb (see section **2.5**) denoting place: *Stand over **there**.*

> *They're* is a contraction of *they are*: *Our guests are early: **they're** here already.*

your/you're:

> *Your* is a possessive pronoun (see section **2.6.2**): ***Your** car has been stolen.*

> *You're* is a contraction of *you are*: ***You're** a good friend.*

Exercises

Exercise 5.1 The structure of words (sections 5.1–5.3)

Analyse the following words in terms of their internal structure, that is, in terms of prefixes, base and suffixes. For example:

unfaithful: un + faith + ful

anti-terrorist	mistreatment	retighten
creativity	naturalism	underdevelopment
deforestation	nonspecialist	ungrateful
disrespectful	profitability	unlawfully
leadership	relentlessly	unremarkable

Exercise 5.2 Adding inflections: general spelling rules (section 5.9)

Form words by joining the parts:

big + est	forget + ing	silly + est
brag + ed	holy + er	simple + est
deal + ing	long + er	slam + ed
defy + ed	move + ing	study + s
enrich + s	rely + ed	untie + ing
fizz + s	revel + ed	watch + s

Exercise 5.3 Adding -ly and -ally (section 5.10)

Convert the following adjectives to adverbs by adding *-ly* or *-ally*:

artistic	guilty	public
automatic	ironic	sadistic
clumsy	lazy	technical
cool	local	temporary
diplomatic	logical	typical
dreadful	lucky	uneasy
energetic	necessary	vital
frantic	nostalgic	voluntary
fundamental	ordinary	
greedy	organic	

Exercise 5.4 Plural nouns (section 5.11)

Give the plural form of the following nouns:

appendix	gallery	pitch
arena	journey	potato
basis	leech	stitch
bush	lorry	studio
cello	mattress	tax
flamingo	medium	taxi
fungus	phobia	wife

Exercise 5.5 Problem spellings (section 5.14)

Fill in the blanks by selecting the correct word from the choices given:

1 The bank refused to . . . the cheque. (*accept/except*)
2 My hotel room was very . . . (*quiet/quite*)
3 We can do nothing to . . . the situation. (*altar/alter*)
4 People should . . . what they preach. (*practice/practise*)
5 He eats everything . . . seafood. (*accept/except*)
6 I left my laptop . . . on the table. (*their/there/they're*)
7 . . . starting to snow. (*its/it's*)
8 It was . . . warm yesterday. (*quiet/quite*)
9 The government could easily . . . the next election. (*loose/lose*)
10 I've got a job interview with the . . . Officer. (*personal/personnel*)
11 The menu is so big I don't know what to . . . (*choose/chose*)
12 Paul told me . . . working from home now. (*your/you're*)
13 The plane lost power in one of . . . engines. (*its/it's*)
14 Amy . . . the dress herself. (*choose/chose*)
15 Our . . . objection is that the ruling is unconsititutional. (*principal/principle*)
16 Parents must face . . . responsibilities. (*their/there/they're*)
17 My son makes more money . . . I do. (*than/then*)
18 We're going to see a marriage guidance . . . (*counsellor/councillor*)
19 Doctors have been studying the . . . of smoking on pregnant women. (*affect/effect*)
20 Your pharmacist will be able to give you . . . (*advise/advice*)

Answers to exercises

Chapter 1

Exercise 1.1 Identifying the Subject (section 1.3)

1 <u>My eldest son</u> graduated in June.
2 <u>The students</u> visited Paris with their teachers.
3 <u>Some flights</u> are very cheap.
4 <u>The concert</u> was very disappointing.
5 At Christmas, <u>most of the children</u> perform in the Nativity Play
6 <u>It</u>'s snowing.
7 <u>It</u> was in June that we met.
8 A year later, <u>Tom and Amy</u> were married.

Exercise 1.2 Identifying the Subject (section 1.3)

1 Is <u>Paul</u> older than Amy?
2 Is <u>lunch</u> ready?
3 Is <u>it</u> cold outside?
4 Is <u>someone</u> watching the house?
5 Has <u>Alan</u> a new car? *or* Does <u>Alan</u> have a new car?
6 Is <u>reading books</u> his favourite pastime?
7 Was <u>it</u> Tom who made the suggestion?
8 Is <u>his Facebook account</u> closed?

Exercise 1.3 Direct Object (section 1.6)

1 The government has promised <u>an end to age discrimination in the workplace</u>.
2 Most people welcomed <u>the government's change of policy</u>.

3 However, some people expressed <u>doubts about the proposed legislation</u>.
4 They are demanding <u>a more comprehensive review of employment law</u>.
5 A Select Committee will discuss <u>the issue</u> next month.
6 The Committee is still accepting <u>submissions</u>.
7 Some people question <u>the need for such extensive consultation</u>.
8 The Opposition will raise <u>the question</u> during the next parliamentary session.

Exercise 1.4 Indirect Object (section 1.7)

1 Send <u>me</u> your email address, please.
2 He owes <u>the bank</u> a lot of money.
3 We've promised <u>Paul</u> a laptop for his birthday.
4 Can you tell <u>us</u> the way to King's Cross?
5 He is teaching <u>the children</u> French.
6 I've emailed <u>you</u> my details.
7 She gave <u>the bridegroom</u> a kiss.
8 They made <u>both candidates</u> the same offer.

Exercise 1.5 Direct Object (section 1.6) and Indirect Object (section 1.7)

She gave <u>Paul</u> (IO) <u>his pocket money</u> (DO).
They paid <u>him</u> (IO) <u>his salary</u> (DO)
Can I ask <u>you</u> (IO) <u>a question</u> (DO)?
They found <u>him</u> (IO) <u>a job at the factory</u> (DO).
The bank charges <u>customers</u> (IO) <u>an annual fee</u> (DO).
She cooked <u>us</u> (IO) <u>a lovely meal</u> (DO).
Show <u>me</u> (IO) <u>your medal</u> (DO).
She always reads <u>the children</u> (IO) <u>a bedtime story</u> (DO).
Have you told <u>Paul</u> (IO) <u>the news</u> (DO)?
They have offered <u>me</u> (IO) <u>the job</u> (DO).
It cost <u>me</u> (IO) <u>a fortune</u> (DO).

Exercise 1.6 Object Complement (section 1.8)

1 Seafood can sometimes make people <u>ill</u>.
2 I usually find science fiction movies <u>very boring</u>.
3 They have named the baby <u>Apple</u>.
4 He proclaimed himself <u>President of the new republic</u>.
5 In 2006, *Time* magazine named him <u>Person of the Year</u>.
6 The alcohol made him <u>drowsy</u>.
7 He was appointed <u>Chief Justice</u> in 2008.
8 He calls himself <u>the king of the jungle</u>.

Exercise 1.7 The six sentence patterns (section 1.10) and Adjuncts (section 1.12)

1 <u>In tropical rainforests</u> (A), <u>bird life</u> (S) is <u>usually</u> (A) <u>very exotic and colourful</u> (SC).
2 <u>The appearance of birds</u> (S) is <u>seasonal</u> (SC).
3 <u>Sometimes</u> (A), <u>the arrival of flowers and fruits</u> (S) will attract <u>birds</u> (DO).
4 <u>The dense canopy of leaves</u> (S) makes <u>the rainforest</u> (DO) <u>very dark</u> (OC).
5 <u>At ground level</u> (A), <u>you</u> (S) can <u>occasionally</u> (A) see <u>kingfishers</u> (DO).
6 <u>The constant gloom and enormous tree trunks</u> (S) give <u>the rainforest</u> (IO) <u>the appearance of a cathedral</u> (DO).
7 The forest stretches <u>three hundred miles eastwards</u> (AC).

Exercise 1.8 Adjuncts (section 1.12)

RMS Titanic left Southampton <u>on 10 April 1912</u>. <u>After crossing the English Channel</u>, she stopped <u>at Cherbourg, France</u>. <u>The next day</u>, she stopped <u>again</u> <u>at Queenstown, Ireland</u>, <u>to allow more passengers to go on board</u>. <u>When she finally sailed to New York</u>, she had 2,240 passengers. <u>On 14 April</u>, <u>just before midnight</u>, the Titanic struck an iceberg <u>in the north Atlantic</u>. The massive ship sank <u>two hours and forty minutes later</u>. <u>As a result</u>, 1,517 people lost their lives. <u>Unfortunately</u>, the owners of the Titanic thought their ship was unsinkable. <u>While they were fitting out the great ship</u>, they did not provide enough lifeboats. <u>Following the sinking</u>, new regulations were introduced, <u>in an effort to ensure that such a catastrophe could never happen again</u>.

Chapter 2

Exercise 2.1 Nouns (section 2.2)

argument
capitalist/capitalism
compensation
criticism
development/developer
disappointment
humiliation/humility
improvisation

intervention
occurrence
offence/offender
perception
reference
requirement
specialist/specialisation
statement

Exercise 2.2 Singular nouns and plural nouns (section 2.2.1)

analyses
bases
bureaux
crises
criteria
formulae

hypotheses
media
phenomena
sisters-in-law
stimuli
wolves

Exercise 2.3 The five verb forms (section 2.3.1)

1 Everyone <u>understands</u> (-s form) the need to <u>reduce</u> (base form) carbon emissions.
2 If you <u>care</u> (base form) about the environment, <u>take</u> (base form) action now.
3 One way we all <u>waste</u> (base form) resources is by <u>leaving</u> (-ing form) lights switched on at home when we're not even there.
4 Governments have only recently <u>realised</u> (-ed form) that carbon emissions <u>threaten</u> (base form) our future.
5 In the 1970s, environmental groups <u>tried</u> (past form) to <u>raise</u> (base form) our awareness of the problem.
6 They have <u>given</u> (-ed form) us a lot to <u>think</u> (base form) about.

Exercise 2.4 Irregular verbs (section 2.3.7)

1 I have **found** a wonderful book on astronomy.
2 He may have **told** his partner.
3 The suspect was **brought** to Paddington police station.
4 Large areas of the coastline were **swept** away by the tsunami.
5 I have been **sworn** to secrecy.
6 He **paid** in cash for a brand-new Porsche.
7 It was **meant** to be a surprise.
8 The castle had **lain** empty for years.
9 The money was **sewn** into the lining of his jacket.
10 The animals were **led** to safety.

Exercise 2.5 Adjectives (section 2.4)

curable	glorious	musical	reasonable
disruptive	legendary	nauseous	religious
drizzly	leaky	peripheral	tedious
geological	massive	questionable	woolly/woollen

Exercise 2.6 Comparative adjectives and superlative adjectives (section 2.4.2)

more brilliant, most brilliant
cleverer, cleverest
more elegant, most elegant
faster, fastest
more handsome, most handsome
luckier, luckiest
warmer, warmest
more wonderful, most wonderful

Exercise 2.7 Adverbs (section 2.5)

absolutely	environmentally	memorably
capably	happily	personally
clearly	lazily	terribly
demonstrably	legally	
dully	luckily	

Exercise 2.8 The meanings of adverbs (section 2.5.4)

1 The choir sang <u>beautifully</u> (M).
2 We'll meet <u>here</u> (P) after the game.
3 Amy works really <u>hard</u> (M) at school.
4 He felt that he had been <u>unfairly</u> (M) treated.
5 Paul doesn't feel well <u>today</u> (T).
6 You can't park <u>there</u> (P).

Exercise 2.9 Pronouns (section 2.6)

1 The banks gave **them** every opportunity to repay the loan.
2 **He** borrowed more money than necessary.
3 He only told **us** about it after he got into financial trouble.
4 Since the financial meltdown, **our** economy has been struggling.
5 The central bank played **its** part in the recovery.
6 The economy of Iceland was badly hit, but **theirs** is a special case.

Exercise 2.10 Pronouns (section 2.6)

1 <u>It</u> (personal) was worst holiday <u>we</u> (personal) ever had.
2 First, <u>our</u> (possessive) luggage went missing.
3 <u>That</u> (demonstrative) was not a good start.
4 Then, <u>our</u> (possessive) taxi driver took <u>us</u> (personal) to the wrong hotel.
5 Then Tom discovered <u>he</u> (personal) had lost <u>his</u> (possessive) passport.
6 So we found <u>ourselves</u> (reflexive) with no luggage, no hotel, and no passport.
7 Eventually, <u>we</u> (personal) phoned the travel agent, <u>who</u> (relative) was very helpful.

Exercise 2.11 Auxiliary verbs (section 2.7)

1 The Internet <u>has</u> (perfective) revolutionised the way we do business.
2 Now we <u>can</u> (modal) order books, theatre tickets and even clothes online.
3 Very soon, every home <u>will</u> (modal) have broadband Internet access.

4   The Internet <u>is</u> (progressive) also changing the way we learn.

5   Online teaching materials <u>can</u> (modal) now <u>be</u> (passive) accessed from anywhere in the world.

6   In the future, all students <u>may</u> (modal) <u>be</u> (passive) taught online.

7   However, some teachers believe this <u>would</u> (modal) be disastrous for students.

8   They say the Internet <u>should</u> (modal) <u>be</u> (passive) used sparingly, and that real teachers <u>can</u> (modal) never <u>be</u> (passive) replaced by computers.

9   For people in remote areas, however, the Internet <u>is</u> (progressive) really improving their access to education.

10   Distance learning <u>has</u> (perfective) finally become a reality.

Exercise 2.12 Words and word classes (Chapter 2)

Howard Carter is <u>famous</u> (Adj) throughout the world as <u>the</u> (Art) man <u>who</u> (Pn) discovered the <u>tomb</u> (N) of the Egyptian king, <u>Tutankamen</u> (N). <u>His</u> (Pn) story <u>is</u> (V) a <u>very</u> (Adv) romantic <u>one</u> (Pn), and it <u>has</u> (Aux) inspired many Hollywood <u>movies</u> (N). Carter <u>was</u> (Aux) born <u>on</u> (P) May <u>9th</u> (Num), 1874, in <u>England</u> (N). His father <u>was</u> (V) an artist <u>who</u> (Pn) specialised in <u>drawing</u> (V) animal portraits <u>for</u> (P) <u>local</u> (Adj) landowners. <u>He</u> (Pn) taught his son the <u>basics</u> (N) of drawing and painting, <u>and</u> (C) Howard <u>became</u> (V) a <u>fairly</u> (Adv) accomplished draughtsman. However, his main interest <u>was</u> (V) in archaeology, and in <u>ancient</u> (Adj) Egypt in particular. <u>When</u> (C) he was just <u>seventeen</u> (Num) years old, Howard sailed <u>to</u> (P) Alexandria in Egypt, <u>hoping</u> (V) to find work as <u>a</u> (Art) draughtsman <u>with</u> (P) the Egyptian Exploration Fund. His <u>first</u> (Num) job was at Bani Hassan, where he worked <u>under</u> (P) the famous <u>archaeologist</u> (N), Flinders Petrie. His role on <u>that</u> (Pn) excavation was to <u>copy</u> (V) the drawings <u>which</u> (Pn) <u>were</u> (Aux) found <u>on</u> (P) the walls of the tombs. <u>According to</u> (P) some sources, Howard worked <u>hard</u> (Adv) all day, and then slept in the tombs <u>at</u> (P) night.

Chapter 3

Exercise 3.1 Noun phrases (section 3.2)

1 [Strong easterly winds]are expected later.
2 [The cost of [insurance]] has doubled in [the last year].
3 [The kids] really enjoyed [their visit to [Disneyland]].
4 [His first movie] was about [the siege of [Krishnapur]].
5 [The weapon] was found at [the bottom of [the lake]].
6 [[Harry Potter] books] are [his favourites].
7 [The concert] was cancelled due to [poor [ticket] sales].
8 [The director of [the company]] has resigned.

Exercise 3.2 Determiners (section 3.2.1)

1 His second attempt at the title was much more successful.
2 Many people expected him to win the first race easily.
3 Some people felt that he needed more time to prepare.
4 One journalist even suggested that he should take a break from all
   competitions.
5 After the second race, he was congratulated by his wife and two
   children.
6 His many loyal fans chanted his name from the grandstand.
7 The fans will remember that victory for many years.
8 For Roberts, it was an emotional climax to a career that began twenty
   years earlier.

Exercise 3.3 The ordering of auxiliary verbs (section 3.3.1)

1 All the tickets have been sold. = Perfective + Passive
2 The prize money will be given to charity. = Modal + Passive
3 The power should be switched off first. = Modal + Passive
4 You must be joking. = Modal + Progressive
5 The earthquake victims are being rehoused. = Progressive + Passive
6 Have you been talking to Paul? = Perfective + Progressive
7 The parents may have been arguing. = Modal + Perfective +
   Progressive
8 Could anything else have been done? = Modal + Perfective + Passive

Exercise 3.4 Tense (section 3.3.2) and Aspect (section 3.3.5)

1 Amy <u>was</u> watching TV when we arrived.
  = Past tense, progressive aspect
2 Paul <u>is</u> working very hard. = Present tense, progressive aspect
3 The government <u>has</u> supported the banks for years.
  = Present tense, perfective aspect
4 I <u>have</u> never met your brother. = Present tense, perfective aspect
5 I <u>am</u> looking for a better job. = Present tense, progressive aspect
6 We <u>were</u> staying with friends at the time.
  = Past tense, progressive aspect
7 The train <u>had</u> already left. = Past tense, perfective aspect
8 All the money <u>has</u> disappeared. = Present tense, perfective aspect

Exercise 3.5 Adjective phrases (section 3.4)

1 In <u>much earlier</u> times, Antwerp had been one of the <u>largest</u> cities in <u>western</u> Europe.
2 The <u>vibrant</u> atmosphere of the <u>sprawling</u> city was <u>very exciting</u> for residents and visitors alike.
3 Antwerp became an <u>increasingly important</u> <u>financial</u> centre as time went on.
4 Prices for works of art were <u>incredibly high</u>, and even <u>fairly mediocre</u> artists could make a <u>reasonably good</u> living.
5 The Church was a <u>very significant</u> contributor to the <u>vast</u> wealth of the city.
6 The Bishop of Antwerp commissioned <u>expensive</u> paintings and statues, and the artists were usually <u>very happy to accept the commissions</u>.
7 The Church had always been <u>acutely aware of the need to patronise artists</u>.
8 In turn, the artists produced some of the <u>most magnificent</u> masterpieces that Europe has ever seen.

Exercise 3.6 Adverb phrases (section 3.5)

1 Global warming has <u>recently</u> become a major concern for governments.
2 <u>Previously</u>, many people felt that governments did not take the issue <u>seriously</u>.
3 <u>Now</u>, it seems that the voice of the people is <u>finally</u> being heard.
4 Governments have <u>gradually</u> realised that climate change is a reality.

5   Some governments are <u>obviously</u> uncertain about how to proceed.

6   Many people feel <u>strongly</u> that international cooperation is the only
solution.

Exercise 3.7 Prepositional phrases (section 3.6)

Marco Polo was born <u>in Venice</u> <u>in 1254</u>. <u>At that time</u>, Venice was one <u>of
Europe's wealthiest cities</u>. <u>At 17</u>, Marco travelled <u>with his father and
uncle</u> <u>from Italy</u> <u>to China</u>. That journey eventually opened trade routes
<u>between the east and the west</u>. <u>In his book</u>, *The Travels of Marco Polo*,
he described the immense size <u>of Chinese cities</u> and the many splendours
to be seen <u>at the Emperor's court</u>. His book contains stories <u>about many
wonders</u>: bandits <u>in desert hideaways</u>, snakes <u>with legs</u>, and an Emperor
who kept a tamed lion <u>at his feet</u>. No one is quite sure how many <u>of
these stories</u> are true. Did he really see everything he described, did he
hear the stories <u>from other travellers</u>, or did he just make it all up? Some
scholars think he never travelled <u>to China</u> <u>at any time</u>. <u>For them</u>, the fact
that he never once mentioned tea, the national drink <u>of the Chinese</u>, is
proof that his book is a collection <u>of fables</u>. <u>Just before his death</u>, Marco
was asked how much <u>of his book</u> was really true. He replied that he had
described only half <u>of what he had actually seen</u>.

Chapter 4

Exercise 4.1 Complex sentences (section 4.1)

1   An earthquake has struck the mountainous region of Qinghai, China,
<u>killing over 600 people.</u>

2   Local authorities estimate <u>that around 9,000 people have been injured</u>.

3   Rescue attempts are difficult <u>because the area is very remote</u>.

4   The disaster struck on Wednesday, <u>when the quake shook the entire
region.</u>

5   Many houses have collapsed in the township of Jiegu, <u>leaving their
occupants homeless</u>.

6   <u>In order to reach some victims</u>, rescuers must tunnel through several
metres of debris.

7   The central government in Beijing has praised the rescuers, <u>who are
working throughout the night</u>.

8   <u>While aftershocks continue</u>, more and more bodies are being found.

Exercise 4.2 Subordinate clause types (section 4.3)

1   The man <u>standing next to the President</u> is his Chief of Staff. **Relative**
2   He is the man <u>who is responsible for all White House staff</u>. **Relative**
3   <u>What every President needs most</u> is someone to organise his timetable.
    Nominal relative
4   President Reagan knew all his staff by their first names, <u>as though he
    had hired them himself</u>. **Adjunct**
5   <u>If the President leaves the White House</u>, he is usually accompanied by
    the press. **Adjunct**
6   President Obama caused panic among security <u>when he slipped out to
    his daughter's football game</u>. **Adjunct**
7   It takes most Presidents some time to learn <u>how to handle all their
    responsibilities</u>. **Nominal relative**

Exercise 4.3 Clauses as sentence elements (section 4.4)

1   That is <u>how most people first get involved with drugs.</u> **Subject
    Complement**
2   Nobody wants <u>to become a drug addict.</u> **Direct Object**
3   Most young people don't even realise <u>that drugs can kill you</u>. **Direct
    Object**
4   For some people, <u>saying 'no'</u> is not as easy as it sounds. **Subject**
5   <u>To avoid conflict at home</u>, some parents just ignore the problem.
    Adjunct
6   <u>To criticise all parents on these grounds</u> is a bit harsh. **Subject**
7   Teenagers simply don't like <u>being criticised</u>. **Direct Object**
8   Uncritical advice is <u>what they need.</u> **Subject Complement**

Exercise 4.4 Clauses as phrase elements (section 4.5)

1   The patient is unable <u>to move his legs</u>. **Postmodifier in an adjective
    phrase**
2   My brother has invented a new way of <u>developing photographs</u>.
    Complement in a prepositional phrase
3   Some children are afraid <u>to go to sleep at night</u>. **Postmodifier in an
    adjective phrase**
4   Following several unsuccessful attempts <u>to restore peace</u>, a ceasefire
    was finally signed. **Postmodifier in a noun phrase**

5   A man <u>who tried to steal a police car</u> has been detained for questioning. **Postmodifier in a noun phrase**
6   The UN considered a suggestion <u>that German soldiers should be part of the peace-keeping troop</u>. **Complement in a noun phrase**
7   All investors are anxious <u>to get their money back</u>. **Postmodifier in an adjective phrase**

Exercise 4.5 The meanings of Adjunct clauses (section 4.6)

1   <u>When the Christmas lights were switched on</u>, everyone gasped in amazement **Time**
2   <u>Though I couldn't see her face</u>, I knew it was Amy. **Concession**
3   Paul has played music <u>since he was six years old</u>. **Time**
4   <u>If anyone phones</u>, say I'm not here. **Condition**
5   I'll make you a veggie burger, <u>since you don't eat meat</u>. **Reason**
6   I read an old copy of Newsweek <u>while I was waiting</u>. **Time**
7   The microphone wasn't working <u>so no one could hear him</u>. **Result**

Exercise 4.6 Coordination (section 4.8)

1   The forensics team examined the evidence <u>carefully</u> and <u>methodically</u>.
2   You will have to wait <u>two</u> or <u>three</u> weeks for a visa.
3   He <u>works during the day</u> and <u>goes to classes at night</u>.
4   You have to consider <u>your own interests </u>and <u>other people's interests</u>.
5   <u>Voting ends at 9 p.m.</u> but <u>the result won't be known for 48 hours</u>.
6   The dog ran <u>out the door</u> and <u>across the road</u>.
7   My car is <u>very old</u> but <u>in good condition</u>.

Exercise 4.7 Referring expressions (section 4.13) and Antecedent agreement (section 4.14)

1   The prize was awarded jointly to <u>Paul and Amy</u>. *They* got exactly equal marks in the exam.
2   Everyone thinks that <u>winning the Lottery</u> would be marvellous, but *it* can also cause a lot of problems.
3   The drug may have <u>some unexpected side effects</u>. *These* may include inflammation and nausea.
4   <u>Countries throughout western Europe closed their airspace</u>. *That* had never happened before.

5   The climbers left most of *their* equipment at a base camp before
    setting out.
6   The customer slowly buttered his toast before spreading *it* lavishly
    with marmalade.
7   The Metropolitan Police and the Serious Fraud Office have uncovered
    between *them* financial malpractice in the gaming industry.

Exercise 4.8 Substitution using so and do (section 4.15)

1   Paul is a teacher and *so* is his wife.
2   Charles was delighted with the gift, and *so* was Amy.
3   Doctors used to drain a patient's blood using leeches, but they don't
    do so any longer.
4   He wanted me to lie about my tax returns, but I was not prepared to
    do so.
5   You can transfer part of the money to a trust fund, if you *so* wish.
6   I was not very happy with the service, and I told them *so*.
7   Macbeth has an extraordinary capacity to delude himself. *So* too has
    Othello.

Exercise 4.9 Postponed Subjects (section 4.18)

1   It is perfectly normal to worry about the future.
2   It is very important that the children should have adequate food and
    clothing.
3   It is unclear at this stage whether or not they qualify for subsidised
    housing.
4   It is now undisputed that climate change is a reality.
5   It is so much more convenient to use an electric blender.

Chapter 5

Exercise 5.1 The structure of words (sections 5.1–5.3)

anti + terror + ist	mis + treat + ment	re + tight + en
creat + iv + ity	natur + al + ism	under + develop + ment
de + forest + ation	non + special + ist	un + grate + ful
dis + respect + ful	profit + abil + ity	un + law + ful + ly
lead + er + ship	relent + less + ly	un + remark + able

Exercise 5.2 Adding inflections: general spelling rules (section 5.9)

biggest	forgetting	silliest
bragged	holier	simplest
dealing	longer	slammed
defied	moving	studies
enriches	relied	untying
fizzes	revelled	watches

Exercise 5.3 Adding -ly and -ally (section 5.10)

artistically	guiltily	publicly
automatically	ironically	sadistically
clumsily	lazily	technically
coolly	locally	temporarily
diplomatically	logically	typically
dreadfully	luckily	uneasily
energetically	necessarily	vitally
frantically	nostalgically	voluntarily
fundamentally	ordinarily	
greedily	organically	

Exercise 5.4 Plural nouns (section 5.11)

appendices	galleries	pitches
arenas	journeys	potatoes
bases	leeches	stitches
bushes	lorries	studios
cellos	mattresses	taxes
flamingoes	media	taxis
fungi	phobias	wives

Exercise 5.5 Problem spellings (section 5.14)

1 The bank refused to **accept** the cheque.
2 My hotel room was very **quiet**.
3 We can do nothing to **alter** the situation.
4 People should **practise** what they preach.

5 He eats everything **except** seafood.

6 I left my laptop **there** on the table.

7 **It's** starting to snow.

8 It was **quite** warm yesterday.

9 The government could easily **lose** the next election.

10 I've got a job interview with the **Personnel** Officer.

11 The menu is so big I don't know what to **choose.**

12 Paul told me **you're** working from home now.

13 The plane lost power in one of **its** engines.

14 Amy **chose** the dress herself.

15 Our **principal** objection is that the ruling is unconsititutional.

16 Parents must face **their** responsibilities.

17 My son makes more money **than** I do.

18 We're going to see a marriage guidance **counsellor.**

19 Doctors have been studying the **effect** of smoking on pregnant women.

20 Your pharmacist will be able to give you **advice.**

Appendix

English irregular verbs

Irregular verbs (see section **2.3.7**) are verbs in which the past form and the -*ed* form are not spelled in the regular way. The 'regular way' adds -*ed* to the base form of the verb (e.g. base form = *walk*, past form = *walked*, -*ed* form = (has) *walked*). Some of the verbs listed here have regular and irregular variants (see section **2.3.8**). On the five verb forms, see section **2.3.1**. For the verb *be*, see section **2.3.9**.

Base form	-s form	Past form	-ed form	-ing form
awake	awakes	awoke	awoken	awaking
bear	bears	bore	borne	bearing
beat	beats	beat	beaten	beating
become	becomes	became	become	becoming
begin	begins	began	begun	beginning
bend	bends	bent	bent	bending
bet	bets	bet	bet	betting
bid	bids	bid	bid	bidding
bind	binds	bound	bound	binding
bite	bites	bit	bitten	biting
bleed	bleeds	bled	bled	bleeding
blow	blows	blew	blown	blowing
break	breaks	broke	broken	breaking
bring	brings	brought	brought	bringing
breed	breeds	bred	bred	breeding
build	builds	built	built	building
burn	burns	burned	burnt	burning

Base form	-s form	Past form	-ed form	-ing form
burst	bursts	burst	burst	bursting
buy	buys	bought	bought	buying
cast	casts	cast	cast	casting
catch	catches	caught	caught	catching
choose	chooses	chose	chosen	choosing
cling	clings	clung	clung	clinging
come	comes	came	come	coming
creep	creeps	crept	crept	creeping
cut	cuts	cut	cut	cutting
deal	deals	dealt	dealt	dealing
dig	digs	dug	dug	digging
dive	dives	dived	dived	diving
do	does	did	done	doing
draw	draws	drew	drawn	drawing
dream	dreams	dreamed	dreamt	dreaming
drink	drinks	drank	drunk	drinking
drive	drives	drove	driven	driving
eat	eats	ate	eaten	eating
fall	falls	fell	fallen	falling
feed	feeds	fed	fed	feeding
feel	feels	felt	felt	feeling
fight	fights	fought	fought	fighting
find	finds	found	found	finding
flee	flees	fled	fled	fleeing
fling	flings	flung	flung	flinging
fly	flies	flew	flown	flying
forget	forgets	forgot	forgotten	forgetting
freeze	freezes	froze	frozen	freezing
get	gets	got	got	getting
give	gives	gave	given	giving
go	goes	went	gone	going

Base form	-s form	Past form	-ed form	-ing form
grind	grinds	ground	ground	grinding
grow	grows	grew	grown	growing
have	has	had	had	having
hear	hears	heard	heard	hearing
hide	hides	hid	hidden	hiding
hit	hits	hit	hit	hitting
hold	holds	held	held	holding
hurt	hurts	hurt	hurt	hurting
keep	keeps	kept	kept	keeping
kneel	kneels	knelt	knelt	kneeling
knit	knits	knitted	knit	knitting
know	knows	knew	known	knowing
lay	lays	laid	laid	laying
lead	leads	led	led	leading
lean	leans	leaned	leant	leaning
leap	leaps	leaped	leapt	leaping
learn	learns	learned	learnt	learning
leave	leaves	left	left	leaving
lend	lends	lent	lent	lending
let	lets	let	let	letting
lie[1]	lies	lay	lain	lying
light	lights	lit	lit	lighting
lose	loses	lost	lost	losing
make	makes	made	made	making
mean	means	meant	meant	meaning
meet	meets	met	met	meeting
pay	pays	paid	paid	paying
prove	proves	proved	proven	proving
put	puts	put	put	putting

1 The verb *lie*, meaning *to tell an untruth*, is a regular verb.

Base form	-s form	Past form	-ed form	-ing form
quit	quits	quit	quit	quitting
read	reads	read	read	reading
ride	rides	rode	ridden	riding
ring	rings	rang	rung	ringing
rise	rises	rose	risen	rising
run	runs	ran	run	running
say	says	said	said	saying
see	sees	saw	seen	seeing
seek	seeks	sought	sought	seeking
sell	sells	sold	sold	selling
send	sends	sent	sent	sending
set	sets	set	set	setting
sew	sews	sewed	sewn	sewing
shake	shakes	shook	shaken	shaking
shine	shines	shone	shone	shining
shoot	shoots	shot	shot	shooting
show	shows	showed	shown	showing
shrink	shrinks	shrank	shrunk	shrinking
shut	shuts	shut	shut	shutting
sing	sings	sang	sung	singing
sink	sinks	sank	sunk	sinking
sit	sits	sat	sat	sitting
sleep	sleeps	slept	slept	sleeping
slide	slides	slid	slid	sliding
smell	smells	smelled	smelt	smelling
speak	speaks	spoke	spoken	speaking
speed	speeds	sped	sped	speeding
spell	spells	spelled	spelt	spelling
spend	spends	spent	spent	spending
spill	spills	spilled	spilt	spilling
spin	spins	spun	spun	spinning

Base form	-s form	Past form	-ed form	-ing form
spit	spits	spat	spat	spitting
split	splits	split	split	splitting
spoil	spoils	spoiled	spoilt	spoiling
spread	spreads	spread	spread	spreading
spring	springs	sprang	sprung	springing
stand	stands	stood	stood	standing
steal	steals	stole	stolen	stealing
stick	sticks	stuck	stuck	sticking
sting	stings	stung	stung	stinging
strike	strikes	struck	struck	striking
string	strings	strung	strung	stringing
strive	strives	strove	striven	striving
swear	swears	swore	sworn	swearing
sweep	sweeps	swept	swept	sweeping
swell	swells	swelled	swollen	swelling
swim	swims	swam	swum	swimming
swing	swings	swung	swung	swinging
take	takes	took	taken	taking
teach	teaches	taught	taught	teaching
tear	tears	tore	torn	tearing
tell	tells	told	told	telling
think	thinks	thought	thought	thinking
throw	throws	threw	thrown	throwing
wake	wakes	woke	woken	waking
wear	wears	wore	worn	wearing
weave	weaves	wove	woven	weaving
weep	weeps	wept	wept	weeping
win	wins	won	won	winning
wind	winds	wound	wound	winding
wring	wrings	wrung	wrung	wringing
write	writes	wrote	written	writing

Glossary of terms

Acronym
A word formed from the initial letters of other words, e.g. *AIDS* (*a*cquired *i*mmune *d*eficiency *s*yndrome).

Active
See **Voice**.

Adjective
Adjectives express a quality or attribute of a noun: *a **happy** child*; *a **violent** storm*; *an **old** car*. Adjectives can also appear after the noun: *the child is **happy***.

Adjective phrase
A phrase in which the main word is an adjective. The adjective may occur on its own in the phrase (***happy**, **old**, **rich***), or it may have a Premodifier before it (*very **happy**, quite **old**, extremely **rich***). Some adjective phrases may also have Postmodifiers after the adjective (***tired** of waiting, **happy** to meet you*).

Adjunct
A grammatically optional element in sentence structure. Adjuncts convey optional, additional information, including when something happened (*Our guests arrived **on Sunday**.*), where something happened (*We met Paul **outside the cinema**.*) and why something happened (*Amy cried **because she lost her doll**.*).

Adjunct clause
A subordinate clause that functions as an Adjunct in sentence structure: *Amy cried **because she lost her doll**; **Although he is poor**, he gives what he can to charity.*

Adverb
Adverbs are used to modify a verb (*Amy sings **beautifully***), an adjective (***extremely** big*) or another adverb (***very** recently*).

Adverb phrase
A phrase in which the main word is an adverb. The adverb may occur on its own (***beautifully**, **recently***) or it may have a Premodifier before it (*very **beautifully**, quite **recently***).

Adverbial Complement
An element that occurs with an intransitive verb and typically expresses location, direction or time: *The road goes **to Sevenoaks**; The play lasted **two hours**.*

Alternative interrogative
A question that offers two or more alternative responses: *Do you want tea or coffee?; Is that William or Harry?* Cf. **Yes–no interrogative**.

Anaphora	The use of a word or words to refer back to something previously mentioned. The personal pronouns are often used anaphorically, as in *James likes football.* ***He*** *never misses a game.* Here, *he* refers anaphorically to *James*. Cf. **Cataphora**.
Antecedent	A word or words to which a following word refers back. In *James likes football.* ***He*** *never misses a game, James* is the antecedent of *he*. Cf. **Anaphora**, **Cataphora**.
Anticipatory *it*	Anticipatory *it* occupies the Subject position in a sentence and 'anticipates' a Subject that has been postponed: ***It*** *is obvious that he doesn't love her.* (Cf. *That he doesn't love her is obvious.*) Cf. **Postponed Subject**.
Apposition	A relationship between two units (usually noun phrases), in which both units refer to the same person or thing: *The President, Mr Obama.*
Article	The articles are *the* (the definite article) and *a/an* (the indefinite article).
Aspect	Aspect expresses how an event is viewed with respect to time. There are two aspects in English, the progressive aspect (*William is leaving/was leaving*) and the perfective aspect (*William has left/had left*).
Asyndetic coordination	Coordination without the use of *and*: *We need* **bread, cheese, eggs, milk, flour.** Cf. **Syndetic coordination**, **Polysyndetic coordination**.
Attributive	A term used to refer to an adjective that occurs immediately before a noun: *the* **new** *car.* Cf. **Postpositive**, **Predicative**.
Auxiliary verb	A 'helping' verb that typically comes before the main verb in a sentence (*I* **can** *drive; James* **has** *written to the Council*). Auxiliary verbs are divided into the following types: modal, passive, progressive, perfective, *do* auxiliary, semi-auxiliary.
Back formation	A verb formed by removing a noun ending and adding a verb ending, e.g. *televise*, from *television*.
Base form	The form of a verb that follows *to*, and to which the inflections are added: *to walk, walk+s, walk+ed, walk+ing*. The term is also used to refer to the uninflected form of an adjective or adverb to which the *-er* and *-est* endings are added. Cf. **Comparative form**, **Superlative form**.
Case	A distinction, chiefly in pronouns, that relates to their grammatical functions. Personal pronouns and the pronoun *who* have two cases: Subjective case (e.g. *I, we, who*) and objective case (*me, us, whom*). Nouns exhibit two cases, the common case (*dog, dogs*) and the genitive case (*dog's, dogs'*).
Cataphora	The use of a word or words to refer forward to a later word: *When you see* **him**, *will you ask* **Simon** *to phone me?* Cf. **Anaphora**.

Clause A sentence-like construction that operates at a level lower than a sentence: *We visited Disneyland **when we were in Hong Kong***. Here, the clause ***when we were in Hong Kong*** is 'sentence-like' in the sense that it has its own Subject (*we*) and its own verb (*were*). However, some clauses may have only an 'implied' Subject: ***Working through the night**, rescuers finally reached the miners*. Here, the 'implied' Subject of the clause *working through the night* is *rescuers*, the Subject of the sentence as a whole.

Cleft sentence A sentence with the pattern *It + be + focus + relative clause*, e.g. *It was William who noticed the error* (cf. *William noticed the error*). Cleft sentences are used to emphasise the focus, here, *William*.

Clipping A type of abbreviation in which one or more syllables are omitted from a word, e.g. *demo*, from *demonstration*.

Closed word class A closed word class is one that does not admit new members. For example, the class of prepositions (*at, in, of*, etc.) does not admit new members and therefore is a closed class. Cf. **Open word class**.

Comment clause A peripheral clause in sentence structure, used to offer a comment on what is being said: *I can't afford it, **I'm afraid***.

Comparative clause Comparative clauses are introduced by *than* and express comparison: *The play was better **than I expected***; *David is stronger **than he used to be***.

Comparative form A term used to refer to the *-er* form of adjectives (*happier*) and adverbs (*sooner*). Cf. **Superlative form**.

Complement A unit that completes the meaning of a word, e.g. a noun (*the fact **that the earth is round***) or a preposition (*under **the table***). The term is also sometimes applied to the Direct Object, which completes the meaning of a transitive verb (*The soldiers destroyed **the village***).

Complex sentence A sentence that contains one or more subordinate clauses: *The match was abandoned **because the pitch was waterlogged***; *The referee decided **to abandon the match***.

Compound sentence A sentence that consists of two or more clauses linked by a coordinating conjunction (*and, but, or*): *Emily works during the day **and** she studies at night*.

Concord Another term for Subject–verb agreement.

Conditional clause A conditional clause is typically introduced by *if* and expresses a condition: ***If we get home early**, we can watch the new DVD*.

Conjoin A term used to described items that are linked by a coordinating conjunction: ***Paul** and **Amy**; **tea** or **coffee**; **tired** but **happy***.

Conjunction	The coordinating conjunctions (*and, but, or*) link elements of equal status: *I play guitar, **and** David sings*. The subordinating conjunctions (e.g. *if, because, since*) introduce a subordinate clause: *Have some pasta **if** you want it.*
Coordination	The linking of two or more units using one of the coordinating conjunctions, *and, but* and *or*: *We bought meat **and** vegetables; David graduated last year **but** he still can't find a job; You don't need money **or** good looks.*
Copular verb	Another term for **linking verb**.
Countable noun	Countable nouns denote things that can be counted: *one chair, two chairs, three chairs* etc. Therefore, they have both a singular form (*chair*) and a plural form (*chairs*). Also called count nouns. Cf. **Uncountable noun**.
Declarative sentence	A sentence that is chiefly used for making a statement: *The sky was blue; William became an engineer; The government has a huge majority*. Cf. **Interrogative sentence**.
Definite article	The definite article is the word *the*.
Demonstrative pronoun	The demonstrative pronouns are *this, that, these* and *those*.
Determiner	Determiners are elements in the structure of a noun phrase. They introduce the noun phrase and typically refer to quantity or position in an ordered sequence: ***a** newspaper; **some** people; **many** problems; **three** ships; **all our** friends, **the first** day*.
Direct Object	The element required by a transitive verb to complete its meaning: *David announced **his retirement**; The company made **a huge profit***. Direct Objects are most commonly noun phrases, but they can also be clauses: *David announced **that he will retire***.
Direct speech	A method of reporting speech in which the actual words that were used are quoted: *'I'm very tired', said James*. Cf. **Indirect speech**.
***Do* auxiliary**	The *do* auxiliary is used (a) to form questions (***Do** you like French films?*); (b) to form negatives, with *not* (*I **do** not enjoy violent films*); (c) to form negative directives, with *not* (***Do** not sit there!*); (d) for emphasis (*I **do** enjoy a good book!*).
Etymology	The study of the origin and history of words.
Exclamative sentence	A sentence that expresses an exclamation: *What a pity! How tall he's grown!*
'Existential' sentence	See ***There*-sentence**.
Finite	If the first (or only) verb in a verb phrase exhibits tense (past or present), then the verb phrase is finite. The following sentences all contain a finite verb phrase: *David left early; David leaves at eight every morning; David is leaving now; David had left*. The term is also applied to clauses in which the verb phrase is finite. Cf. **Non-finite**.

Form	In grammatical descriptions, the term *form* refers to the structure, appearance or 'shape' of an element. For instance, we say that the adjective *old* has three forms, *old, older, oldest*. Cf. **Function**.
Fragment	An incomplete sentence, often used in response to a question: *Where did you leave the keys?* **On the table**. Fragments are normally interpreted as if they were complete sentences: *I left the keys on the table*. Cf. **Non-sentence**.
Function	The grammatical role that an element performs in a sentence, clause or phrase. For instance, in *The old man is ill*, the element *the old man* performs the function of Subject. In turn, the adjective *old* performs the function of Premodifier in the noun phrase *the old man*. Cf. **Form**.
Gender	A term used to refer to grammatical distinctions based on differences in sex: *he/she, his/her*.
Gradability	Gradable words are adjectives and adverbs that can be modified by an intensifier: *fairly* **cold**; *very* **cold**; *extremely* **cold**; and that have comparative and superlative forms: *cold, colder, coldest*.
Imperative sentence	A type of sentence used in giving orders: *Move over, Come in, Don't leave your coat there*.
Indefinite article	The indefinite article is *a/an*.
Indirect Object	Some transitive verbs require two elements to complete their meaning: *We gave James a gift*. Here, *James* is the Indirect Object, and *a gift* is the Direct Object. The Indirect Object typically refers to the person who receives something or benefits from the action expressed by the verb.
Indirect speech	Indirect speech reports what has been said, but not in the actual words used by the speaker: *James said that he was very tired*. Compare: *'I'm very tired', said James*, which is **direct speech**.
Infinitive	The base form of a verb when it is introduced by *to*: *She loves* **to sing**; *They decided* **to cooperate**.
Inflection	An ending that indicates a grammatical category. For instance, the *-s* inflection when added to a noun indicates plural number.
Intensifier	A type of adverb used to express degree in an adjective or in another adverb. The most common intensifier is *very*: **very** *cold*; **very** *recently*. Other intensifiers include *extremely, fairly, highly, quite*.
Interrogative sentence	A type of sentence used in asking questions: *Is James here? Did you have a good time? What is this? How is the patient?*
Intransitive verb	A verb that requires no other element to complete its meaning: *David* **slept**; *It is still* **snowing**. Cf. **Transitive verb**.
Linking verb	The most common linking verb is *be*: *My uncle* **is** *a professional footballer*. Linking verbs link the Subject (*my uncle*) with the Subject Complement (*a professional footballer*). Other linking verbs include *seem* (*He* **seems** *angry*.) and *appear* (*She* **appears** *distracted*).

Main clause	A clause that can stand independently. In ***Emily worked in Greece*** *when she was young*, the main clause is *Emily worked in Greece*. The second clause, *when she was young*, can be omitted and is a subordinate clause.
Main verb	In the verb phrase *was raining*, *raining* is the main verb, while *was* is the auxiliary verb.
Mass noun	Another term for **uncountable noun**.
Modal auxiliary	The modal auxiliary verbs are *can, could, may, might, must, shall, should, will, would*.
Mood	A grammatical category that indicates the attitude of the speaker to what is said. English has three moods: indicative, imperative, subjunctive.
Morphology	The study of the structure of words.
Multi-word verb	A combination consisting of a verb and one or two other words, acting as a unit. Multi-word verbs include prepositional verbs (*look at, rely on*), phrasal verbs (*give in, take over*) and phrasal-prepositional verbs (*look forward to, put up with*).
Nominal relative clause	A subordinate clause introduced by *what, whatever, whoever, where*: ***What you need*** *is a long holiday; I can't understand **what he is saying**; I'll speak to **whoever is responsible***.
Non-finite	If the first (or only) verb in a verb phrase has the base form (*Simon is reluctant **to make an effort**), the -ing form (**Working hard** brings its own reward*) or the -ed form (***Published in 1998**, it soon became a best-seller*), then the verb phrase is non-finite. The term is also used to describe a clause containing a non-finite verb phrase. Cf. **Finite**.
Non-restrictive relative	A 'non-defining' relative clause that simply adds information: *The passenger, **who was about 20**, was not injured*. Compare the 'defining' restrictive relative clause: *The passenger **who was in the rear seat** was not injured*.
Non-sentence	An independent unit that has no sentence structure. Non-sentences are commonly used in public signs and notices: *Motorway Ahead; 10% Off*. Cf. **Fragment**.
Noun	Common nouns are the names of objects (*book, computer*), people (*boy, father*), states (*loneliness, happiness*), abstract concepts (*history, honesty*) etc. Proper nouns refer to individual people (*Nelson Mandela, Winston Churchill*), places (*London, Hong Kong*) and geographical features (*Mount Everest, River Thames*).
Noun phrase	A phrase in which the main word is a noun. The noun may occur on its own (*children, water*), or it may have a Premodifier before it (*young children, cold water*). A noun phrase may also contain a Postmodifier after the noun (***children** with learning disabilities, **cold water** from the stream*). A noun phrase may be introduced by a determiner (***the** children, **some** water*).

169

Number contrast	The contrast between singular and plural, e.g. *dog/dogs, woman/women, this/these.*
Object	See **Direct Object, Indirect Object.**
Object Complement	A sentence element that denotes an attribute of the Object. For instance, in *The dye turned the water blue, blue* denotes the colour of *the water* (the Object), and so *blue* is the Object Complement.
Objective case	The objective case of a personal pronoun is used when the pronoun is a Direct Object (*Simon met **me***) or an Indirect Object (*Simon bought **me** a ticket*). It is also used after a preposition (*Simon bought a ticket for **me***). Cf. **Subjective case.**
Open word class	An open word class is one that admits new members as the need arises. The major open classes are nouns and main verbs. Cf. **Closed word class.**
Parenthetical	A complete sentence inserted in another sentence: *The merger – **this is confidential** – will go ahead as planned.*
Participial adjective	An adjective with an *-ed* ending (*a **dedicated** worker*) or an *-ing* ending (*a **surprising** result*).
Participle	The *-ed* and *-ing* forms of a verb. In some grammars, these are called the *-ed* participle (or 'past participle') and the *-ing* participle (or 'present participle').
Passive	See **Voice.**
Perfective auxiliary	The perfective auxiliary is *have.* It occurs before the *-ed* form of a main verb: *Simon **has** arrived; We **had** hoped you could come.*
Person	A grammatical category that indicates a relationship with the speaker: **first person** refers to the speaker (*I, me*), **second person** refers to the addressee (*you*), and **third person** refers to all others (*they, them*)
Personal pronoun	The personal pronouns are *I/me, you, he/him, she/her/it, we/us, they/them.* See **Subjective case, Objective case.**
Phrasal verb	See **Multi-word verb.**
Phrasal–prepositional verb	See **Multi-word verb.**
Polysyndetic coordination	Coordination in which *and* or *or* is used between each pair of coordinated items: *The lecture went on **and** on **and** on; You can have pasta **or** meatloaf **or** salad.* Cf. **Asyndetic coordination, Syndetic coordination.**
Possessive pronoun	The possessive pronouns are *my/mine, your/yours, his, her/hers/its, our/ours, their/theirs.*

Postmodifier
A phrase or clause that comes after a word and modifies or specifies its meaning: *the man* **behind me***; the man* **who lives beside us***; scared* **of dogs***; afraid* **to cross the street***.*

Postponed Subject
A Subject that has been postponed to the end of a sentence, with the normal Subject position filled by anticipatory *it*: *It is surprising* **that no one claimed the reward** (cf. **That no one claimed the reward** *is surprising*).
Cf. **Anticipatory it.**

Postpositive
A term used to refer to an adjective that occurs immediately after a noun: *the person* **responsible***.* Cf. **Attributive, Predicative.**

Predicate
Everything in a sentence excluding the Subject: *David* (Subject) *won a scholarship* (Predicate).

Predicative
A term used to refer to an adjective that occurs in the Predicate of a sentence, after the verb: *The car is* **new***.*
Cf. **Attributive, Postpositive.**

Prefix
A sequence of letters, such as *un-* (*unlawful*), *anti-* (*anti-abortion*), *post-* (*post-war*), added to the beginning of a word to form a new word. Cf. **Suffix.**

Premodifier
A phrase that comes before a word and modifies or specifies its meaning: *an* **extremely old** *building*; **very** *recently.*

Preposition
Common prepositions include *after, at, before, beside, for, in, of, under, with.* Prepositions are used to introduce a noun phrase: **after** *the ballet*; **at** *the supermarket*; **before** *breakfast.*

Prepositional Complement
The element (usually a noun phrase) that is introduced by a preposition: *after* **the ballet***; under* **our roof***, in* **New York***, at* **ten o'clock***.*

Prepositional phrase
A phrase that is introduced by a preposition. The preposition is followed by a Prepositional Complement, which is usually a noun phrase: *after the ballet*; *under our roof*; *in New York*; *at ten o'clock.*

Prepositional verb
See **Multi-word verb.**

Progressive auxiliary
The progressive auxiliary *be* occurs before a main verb with *-ing* form: *I* **am** *organising a trip to Paris*; *Paul* **is** *collecting money for charity*; *The children* **were** *shouting.*

Pronoun
Pronouns are divided into the following main classes: **demonstrative, gender-neutral, personal, possessive, reflexive.**

Pseudo-coordination
The use of coordinating conjunctions *and* and *or* without any real coordinating function: *Please try* **and** *come early*; *It's a satellite navigation system,* **or** *SatNav.* Cf. **Coordination.**

Reason clause
A reason clause is typically introduced by *because* and expresses the reason why something takes place: *The farmers abandoned the land* **because it was contaminated***.*

171

**Reduced
relative clause**

A relative clause in which the relative pronoun is
omitted, and the verb has -ed form or -ing form: *Films* **produced
on a small budget** *are rarely successful* (compare: *Films* **which
are produced on a small budget**); *The man* **standing beside
you** *is my uncle* (compare: *The man* **who is standing beside
you**).

**Reflexive
pronoun**

The reflexive pronouns are *myself, yourself, himself, herself,
itself, ourselves, yourselves, themselves.*

Relative clause

A relative clause is introduced by a relative pronoun such as
who, which or *that*: *The man* **who lives beside us** *is unwell*; *It's a
new company* **which specialises in web design**; *The project* **that
I'm working on** *is really interesting.*

Relative pronoun

The relative pronouns are *who(m), whose, which* and *that*. They
are used to introduce a relative clause: *The man* **who lives
beside us** *is unwell.*

Reporting clause

A clause such as *he said*, or *said Mary*, that identifies the speaker
of direct speech: *'I'm leaving now'*, **he said**.

**Restrictive
relative clause**

A defining relative clause that identifies the noun
preceding it: *The passenger* **who was in the rear seat** *was not
injured.* Cf. **Non-restrictive relative clause.**

Semantics

The study of the relationship between linguistic forms and
meaning.

Semi-auxiliary

A multi-word auxiliary verb. Examples include *have to* (*I* **have
to** *catch a bus*), *be going to* (**He's going to** *fall*) and *be about to*
(*The factory* **is about to** *close*).

**Sentential
relative clause**

A relative clause that expresses a comment on what
has previously been said: *Amy can't come this evening*, **which is
a pity**.

Simple sentence

A sentence that contains no subordinate clause.

Subject

The sentence element that typically comes before the verb in
a declarative sentence: **James** (S) *is* (V) *still at school.* In an
interrogative sentence, the Subject and the verb change places
with each other: *Is* (V) **James** (S) *still at school?*

**Subject
Complement**

The sentence element that completes the meaning of a
linking verb (usually *be*): *Paul* **is my nephew**; *Our house* **is too
small**; *The weather* **was beautiful**.

Subjective case

The Subjective case of a personal pronoun is used when the
pronoun acts as Subject: **I** *met Simon*, in contrast with the
objective case: *Simon met* **me**.

**Subject–verb
agreement**

A term used to denote the fact that a verb form agrees in
number (singular or plural) with its Subject (compare: *The dog*
barks/*The dogs* **bark**). Subject–verb agreement applies only to
present-tense verbs. Also known as **concord.**

Subjunctive

A term used to denote sentences that express a hypothetical
or non-factual situation: *If I* **were** *you, I would invest the money*;

*The Report recommended that the police officers **be** suspended
immediately.*

Subordinate clause	A dependent clause within a larger structure (*John said* **that Mary is leaving**). Here, the subordinate clause is introduced by the subordinating conjunction *that*.
Subordinating conjunction	A word that introduces a subordinate clause. Common subordinating conjunctions include: *although, because, if, since, that, when, while*. Multi-word subordinating conjunctions include *as long as, as though, provided that, rather than*.
Subordination	A relationship between two clauses in which one clause is grammatically dependent on the other. Subordination is often overtly indicated by the use of a subordinating conjunction: *William studied architecture **while he was in Germany***.
Suffix	An ending added to a word to create another word. Noun suffixes include *-ness* (*coolness, kindness*) and *-ism* (*capitalism, optimism*). Adjective suffixes include *-able* (*profitable, reasonable*) and *-al* (*accidental, musical*).
Superlative form	A term used to refer to the *-est* form of adjectives (*happiest*) and adverbs (*soonest*). Cf. **Comparative form**.
Syndetic coordination	Coordination using *and, but* or *or*: *Paul **and** Amy; tired **but** happy; tea **or** coffee*. Cf. **Asyndetic coordination, Polysyndetic coordination**.
Syntax	The study of the arrangement of words in a sentence.
Tag question	A question that is appended to a statement: *You went to Harvard, **didn't you?**; You're not leaving, **are you?***
Tense	There are two tenses in English: the past tense and the present tense. Tense is denoted by the form of the verb: *David **walks** to school* (present tense); *David **walked** to school* (past tense).
***That*-clause**	A subordinate clause introduced by the subordinating conjunction *that*: *Everyone knows **that smoking is dangerous***.
***There*-sentence**	A sentence introduced by *there*, followed, usually, by the verb *be*: ***There is** a fly in my soup*; ***There is** something wrong with the printer*. Also called an **existential sentence**.
Transitive verb	A verb that requires another element to complete its meaning: *Paul **makes** model airplanes; David **bought** a boat*. Cf. **Intransitive verb**.
Uncountable noun	A noun that denotes things which are considered as indivisible wholes (*furniture, mud, software*) and therefore cannot be counted (*two furnitures, *three muds, *four softwares* etc.). Uncountable nouns have a singular form (*software*), but no plural form (**softwares*). Cf. **Countable noun**.
Verb	Verbs are divided into two types: (a) main verbs, such as *break, buy, eat, sing, write,* and (b) auxiliary verbs, such as *can, could, may, must, might, shall, should, will, would*.

173

Verb phrase — A phrase in which the main word is a verb. The verb may occur on its own (*walked*, *sings*), or it may be preceded by one or more auxiliary verbs (*has walked*, *can walk*, *has been singing*).

Verbless clause — A subordinate clause that lacks a main verb: ***Though poor***, *he gives what he can to charity* (cf. *Though he **is** poor . . .*).

Voice — A term used to describe the contrast between an active sentence – *The police arrested the suspect* – and a passive sentence – *The suspect was arrested (by the police)*.

Vocative — A noun phrase used to identify the person or persons being addressed: *Come in,* ***Dr Johnson***; ***Paul***, *where have you been?*; *Stop arguing,* ***you guys***.

Wh*-interrogative** — A question introduced by *who*, *what*, *where*, *when* or *how*: ***Who *was at the door?* ***What*** *would you like to drink?* ***Where*** *are my keys?* ***When*** *is your flight?* ***How*** *do you switch it on?*

***Yes–no* interrogative** — A question that normally expects an answer that is either *yes* or *no*: *Did you enjoy the film? – Yes/No*. Cf. **Alternative interrogative**.

Zero relative clause — A relative clause from which the relative pronoun has been omitted.: *This is the book* ***William recommended***. Cf. *This is the book* ***that/which William recommended***.

Zero subordinate clause — A subordinate clause from which the subordinating conjunction *that* has been omitted: *He must think* ***I'm a fool***. Cf. *He must think* ***that I'm a fool***.

Further reading

Biber, Douglas, Geoffrey Leech and Susan Conrad (2002) *Longman student grammar of spoken and written English*. London: Longman.

Borjars, Kersti and Kate Burridge (2010) *Introducing English grammar*. 2nd edn. London: Hodder Education.

Chalker, Sylvia and Edmund Weiner (1998) *The Oxford dictionary of English grammar*. Oxford: Oxford Paperbacks.

Collins, Peter and Carmella Hollo (2009) *English grammar: an introduction*. 2nd edn. London: Palgrave Macmillan.

Crystal, David (2003) *The Cambridge encyclopedia of the English language*. 2nd edn. Cambridge: Cambridge University Press.

Crystal, David (2004) *Making sense of grammar*. London: Longman.

Crystal, David (2004) *Rediscover grammar*. 2nd edn. London: Longman.

Greenbaum, Sidney (1996) *The Oxford English grammar*. Oxford: Oxford University Press.

Greenbaum, Sidney and Gerald Nelson (2009) *An introduction to English grammar*. 3rd edn, London: Longman.

Greenbaum, Sidney and Edmund Weiner (2000) *The Oxford reference grammar*. Oxford: Oxford University Press.

Huddleston, Rodney and Geoffrey K. Pullum (2005) *A student's introduction to English grammar*. Cambridge: Cambridge University Press.

Hurford, James (1994) *Grammar: a student's guide*. Cambridge: Cambridge University Press.

Leech, Geoffrey and Jan Svartvik (2003) *A communicative grammar of English*. 3rd edn. London: Longman.

Nelson, Gerald and Justin Buckley (1998) *The Internet grammar of English*. Survey of English Usage, University College London. Available online at www.ucl.ac.uk/internet-grammar/.

Seely, John (2007) *Oxford A-Z of grammar and punctuation*. Oxford: Oxford University Press.

Trask, R. L. (1993) *A dictionary of grammatical terms in linguistics*. London and New York: Routledge.

Index